Also edited by Robert Gathorne-Hardy

Memoirs of Lady Ottoline Morrell:
A Study in Friendship 1873–1915

This is a Borzoi Book, published in New York by
Alfred A. Knopf, Inc.

OTTOLINE
AT GARSINGTON
Memoirs of Lady Ottoline Morrell
1915–1918

OTTOLINE
AT GARSINGTON

Memoirs of
Lady Ottoline Morrell
1915-1918

EDITED WITH AN INTRODUCTION BY
Robert Gathorne-Hardy

Alfred A. Knopf, New York, 1975

THIS IS A BORZOI BOOK
PUBLISHED BY ALFRED A. KNOPF, INC.

Copyright © 1974 by Julian Vinogradoff
Preface, Introduction, and Appendix © 1974 by
The Estate of Robert Gathorne-Hardy
All rights reserved under International and
Pan-American Copyright Conventions.
Published in the United States by
Alfred A. Knopf, Inc., New York,
Distributed by Random House, Inc., New York.
Originally published in Great Britain by
Faber and Faber Limited, London.

Library of Congress Cataloging in Publication Data

Morrell, Ottoline Violet Anne Cavendish-Bentinck, Lady,
1873-1938.
Ottoline at Garsington: Memoirs of Lady Ottoline
Morrell, 1915-1918.
Continues Memoirs of Lady Ottoline Morrell.
Includes index.
1. Morrell, Lady Ottoline Violet Anne Cavendish-Ben-
tinck, 1873-1938. 2. England—Intellectual life—20th
century. I. Title.
DA566.9.M63A36 1975 941.083'092'4 [B] 75-8253
ISBN 0-394-49636-1

Manufactured in the United States of America

First American Edition

Literature is an objective and projected result.
It is Life that is the unconscious, the agitated,
the struggling, the floundering cause.

HENRY JAMES

Contents

Contents

PART TWO

Contents

Preface by Robert Gathorne-Hardy

The first volume of Lady Ottoline Morrell's memoirs was published in 1963. An explanation is needed for the long delay in publishing the second and final volume.

I was the first literary trustee appointed by her. To me she added three others, though I was always her choice as editor. At the time of her death it was clear that nothing could be published for many years without causing pain to people still alive, or to friends of people recently dead. To mutilate the work was unthinkable.

One trustee, just after the War, went around saying that those criticized by Ottoline had treated her badly and did not deserve consideration; the memoirs, he declared, should be published as soon as possible. This came to the knowledge of Bertrand Russell who, I learnt, was much disturbed by the prospect.

At that time I was seeing a great deal of Alys, his first wife and sister of Logan Pearsall Smith. I asked her advice as to whether I should write to Russell (I had been slightly acquainted with him for more than twenty years), and assure him that I had no intention of publishing the memoirs for some considerable time. Indeed, as I said in my preface to the first volume, I had been wondering whether it might not be my duty to edit the text, with such notes and elucidations as I (and often, only I) could supply, and leave the work to be published after my death. I wrote on these lines to Bertrand Russell, who answered that not only would it be unpleasant to see certain passages published (which he knew must exist),—but that it might also be distressing for his wife if, after his death, they were published while she was alive. Accordingly, in the first volume, I suppressed these particular passages. This delicacy, as it turned out, was uncalled for. During his own lifetime he published a full account of his relations with Ottoline, and I was free to print her version of the story, which appears now as an appendix to the present volume.

As will be found, five people were concerned during the troubles over the separation—Bertrand Russell; his wife Alys and her brother Logan Pearsall Smith; Ottoline and Philip Morrell. Of these five, I knew the last four intimately. It is not unlikely that in this I have always been unique; it is quite certain that I am the only person alive with these qualifications. I have used my consequent knowledge in binding together the passages which record all the difficulties of this tumultuous occasion.

I am bound to say here that there are people, for whom I have great affection and great respect, who believe and feel that these passages should not yet be made public. I must therefore categorically affirm that I alone am responsible for the publication. If the act be culpable I, and only I, am to be blamed.

I must repeat here what I said in my preface to the first volume. The whole work is too large for publication, and I have sometimes made large excisions when I believed that in doing so no damage was being done to the historical value of the work. She was apt to be prolix in her writing, and I have occasionally cut phrases and sentences which added to the length, but not to the lucidity of some paragraph. And, as before, I have cut a few passages which could distress people alive, or those close to people not long dead. These occasions are diminishing with the lapse of time.

As will be discovered, the work was never finished. The memoirs end in 1918, before the War was over. (I remember her telling me how they celebrated the peace at Garsington. She put candles in every window of the house, at last uncurtained, and, describing it, remarked on the beauty of the gentle illumination. It may seem strange to later generations that during the 1914–18 War a strict black-out was enforced.) It must have been in 1919 that I first saw her, as I have described, walking up the High Street at Eton. I first met her in 1922. Her memoirs are followed by a gap of about four years to the beginning of the personal and necessarily brief portrait which I wrote as an introduction to the first volume.

Aldous Huxley, Frieda Lawrence and Middleton Murry gave Mrs. Igor Vinogradoff permission to print letters of which they owned the copyright. Of living persons to be thanked are Countess Russell and the literary trustees of the Bertrand Russell estate for permission to print letters of his; Mr. George Sassoon for permission to print writings of his father, Siegfried Sassoon;

and Mrs. Barbara Strachey Halpern for permission to print three letters of her great-aunt, Alys Russell.

I must, as before, thank for her help Mrs. Igor Vinogradoff, the Julian of the memoirs; and it would be churlish not to mention the help and advice I have had from my old friend Mr. Richard de la Mare.

Introduction

by Robert Gathorne-Hardy

When I was planning the first volume of these memoirs, I considered an introduction or an appendix discussing the derisive and derogatory comments about Ottoline which had appeared in various publications. My intention was to examine these, not with indignation but so as to demonstrate factually their demonstrable untruthfulness. I discussed this with her daughter, Mrs. Igor Vinogradoff, and we decided that it would be better to let her speak for herself.

When the book appeared our resolution seemed to have been justified. Osbert Sitwell wrote to me and said that on reading her memoirs he liked her better than he had ever done before. A number of critics wrote about the maliciously selected comments of Virginia Woolf, and the unpleasant observations of Lytton Strachey. Our decision, we felt, was justified. And then was published the life of Lytton Strachey by Mr. Michael Holroyd.

I have, in the first volume of these memoirs, proclaimed the depth of my love for Ottoline. It might be suspected that, in critically examining the character whom Mr. Holroyd presents in her place, I am defending passionately, though perhaps not wisely, the unhappy portrayal of one who was among the dearest of my friends. This is not so. I intend to demonstrate in a few typical cases the general undependability, and often the untruthfulness of the evidence on which Mr. Holroyd had relied.

To guess the workings of another's mind will at best be hypothetical. I can only say what appears most plausible to me. Mr. Holroyd must have read, with an assiduity beyond praise, everything he could find about Strachey and his friends. Of Ottoline he could at first learn little save from the diary of Virginia Woolf, and in the published recollections of other writers. From these, I suspect, he conceived so deeply, so ineradicably, the caricature which he presents in his book, that he could not demolish it when he read her memoirs (and, dare I add, my portrait of her which appears in that volume?); nor did he succeed in reconciling this caricature with the true character to whom Strachey wrote the many serious letters which are quoted. It was to her that he fled for comfort in the misery inflicted on him by Henry Lamb; to her he went for peace, exhausted after his appearance at the tribunal for conscientious objectors.

It would be tedious to examine every misleading source, but I will mention, without naming him, one writer who infected Mr. Holroyd's vision, and whom he quotes. Mr. Holroyd says of him that he 'used to observe her sporting a shepherd's crook with a number of Pekinese dogs attached to it by ribbons'. (Notice the imperfect tense, 'used to observe', implying a continual or repeated process.) It is possible, I suppose, that in earlier times at Garsington, there may have been a shepherd's crook, lost and mouldering in some outhouse; Ottoline was never seen with one. But this quotation refers, in any case, to Gower Street days. There were never more than two dogs there, and they were never attached by ribbons to anything at all, be it walking-stick, gate-post or imaginary shepherd's crook. The same writer, it may be added, describes the entrance of the house with strange in-accuracy and, in his narrative, hangs the walls with paintings of two artists whose works had never been seen there.

Virginia Woolf may seem a larger obstacle. Yet—as Mr. Holroyd himself states—she was a notorious mischief-maker. She had, as I discovered in my slight, bewitched acquaintance with her, an almost uncanny power of opening one's brains and lips. When alone with one other person, and discussing a mutual friend, this gift became dangerous. Logan Pearsall Smith told me that after such an occasion it was the regular practice to go to the victim—the person discussed—and say, 'I've been talking about you to Virginia. I said this, and this, and this. . . . If she tells you I said anything else, it's untrue.' To Mr. Cyril Connolly, Logan told how she would 'lure people to assent to her opinion of her friends and then repeat them as their own'.

She tended to be jealous of noticeable women. She confessed to Ottoline that during the life of Katherine Mansfield she could hardly, from jealousy, read her books. Ottoline was—need it be said?—a noticeable woman, with many friends in Virginia Woolf's world. What she wrote derogatively about Ottoline in her diary has much relevance to her own character, but to Ottoline's very little.

Of Strachey I find it painful to write. I first met him in about 1922. I stayed a number of times at Garsington when he was another guest; often I met him in London, not only at Ottoline's, but when I was working there in the twenties. When I settled in the country, I was about twenty miles from Ham Spray, and used not infrequently to go there while he, though less often, would come to my home (I remember a tea-party about Christmas time when he was induced to pull crackers and wear a paper hat). I was not among his more intimate friends, but I knew him well over a good many years, and I had a strong affection for him. Sadly, in his biography, I discovered ugly traits which I could never have guessed from my memories of the friend.

I will first mention a revealing example of his untrustworthiness which has no connection with Ottoline. In 1921 he stayed with Berenson at his house outside Florence. Two letters which he wrote there are quoted. In one he speaks of 'some female secretaries (I gather)' as being in the party. In the next letter he speaks of everything as dead—'pictures, furniture, servants, books, the Tuscan landscape'—and says, 'The mere fact that he has accumulated this wealth from having been a New York guttersnipe is sufficiently astonishing'.

Among the presumed 'female secretaries' was Nicky Mariano, who would be reckoned by all of her acquaintances as among the most angelic characters they had ever known; for the servants, most had been in the household from the beginning, and were to remain there for decades; the 'dead books' were part of a library which was coming to be among the finest ever contrived by an intelligent man; 'dead pictures' made up an assembly of incomparably beauty: the 'dead Tuscan landscape' was the northern flank of the Val d'Arno. As for the New York guttersnipe, Strachey, having for sister-in-law a step-daughter of Berenson's must have known accurately the facts of his career. It would be difficult to crowd more untruthfulness into so small a space.

It is perhaps relevant to record that I once heard Berenson say of Strachey, 'I think he was the most ill-mannered person I ever met.' Evidently the two men had not hit it off, and Strachey had relieved himself with these two letters.

It would need too much space to consider all the untruths told about Ottoline in his letters. He mentions, in one of them, meeting, at Garsington, Dr. Marten of Freiburg in Breisgau; in the first volume I have told how Ottoline went to be treated by him, and how my friend Kyrle Leng followed. Later, Edward Sack-ville-West arrived. They had all gone to be treated for internal complaints; to his purely medical treatment, Dr. Marten added, of his own choice, a little peremptory psychoanalysis. Strachey reported that psychoanalysis was what they all went for, and that Sackville-West had gone in the hope of being cured of homo-sexual tendencies. There is no truth in this. They went to be treated medically for internal physical illness (my friend for duodenal ulcers).

These two examples are enough—more can easily be found—to establish that Strachey, in his correspondence to certain people, is not to be relied on as a witness. What was the reason for this from almost the most eminent in a group of eminent and remarkable people, who professed to worship truth?

Mr. Holroyd tells of an occasion when, after being with Ottoline, he had praised her to Duncan Grant and Vanessa Bell, 'She was majestic! She was splendid! Magnificent! Sublime!' They deprecated such enormous praise, and he gradually turned until he gave an opinion which, one cannot help but feel, he believed to be more in accordance with their opinion than with his own. It is legitimate to surmise that when, while staying with Ottoline, he wrote unpleasantly (and inaccurately) about her to Virginia Woolf, he was writing, not what he himself truly felt, but what he reckoned the recipient would like to hear. In fact he could lamentably be what we call—there is no other word for it —a toady.

It is thus that Mr. Holroyd has put together from false evi-dence a false picture of Ottoline and has given to her career a shape which, were he writing fiction, would have been admirably contrived. She is a rather comical foil to the more substantial character in his story.

There is first the glory and splendour of Bedford Square, but with already a worm in the wood. Then there is a small decline, always continuing, at Garsington. And there, in 1923 (when I knew it), he detects no more than 'some afterglow of its old magical enchantment'—an assessment which will seem very strange to anybody who knew the place in those days. And it was then, and for several years after, that I witnessed at Garsington the intimate friendship persisting warmly between her and Strachey.

The fiction recedes even further from reality when the

Morrells moved finally to Gower Street. There she is described as 'the faded relic of a great hostess'. The only evidence given for this is that Strachey, meeting James Stephens there, didn't enjoy it. Other guests, myself among them, were less fastidious; we liked the little Irish poet.

The exuberant glories of Bedford Square could not, it is true, be revived. The original participants were twenty years or more older; war had intervened; the world was altogether different. And as for the decline from Garsington, a tea or a luncheon party must be very different from a visit of a week-end or longer, when the guests become for a time members of the household. For all the joy I had in her, and pleasure in the company, I always, in Gower Street, found myself lamenting Garsington. But the decline was no more than a consequence of physical circumstances.

After the appearance of Mr. Holroyd's *Lytton Strachey*, a letter was published expostulating against his general portrayal of Ottline, and in particular against his treatment of her life in Gower Street. Among the signatories was Lord David Cecil who, when a draft of the letter was sent to him, advised adding this sentence; 'an original and imaginative personality as distinguished in her own way as any of her guests were in theirs'. This interpolation was approved by all the signatories.

The substitute of a fictional character for the real Ottoline has unbalanced the history of Strachey's life. According to his biographer, the confidants in the joys and troubles of his love life were, in turn, Maynard Keynes, James Strachey and, in the end, Mrs. St. John Hutchinson. At times Ottoline was equally important in this role, as in the case of his disaster with Henry Lamb. This is recorded in the first volume of her memoirs, which was published before the biography.

The consequences were unfortunate. The attempt to force this false character into the scheme has dislocated the history of Strachey's life, and misled its author in almost every judgement relating to her. His sub-plot of Ottoline's career is of one who attained an all but supreme position as an intellectual hostess, a position which gradually decayed into pathetic insignificance. Given only the evidence which he used the picture is not indefensible. That evidence deceived him, and apparently induced him to emphasize the imaginary situations of an imaginary character. He refers to 'poor Ottoline', or to this 'unhappy woman'; nothing is told to justify his adjectives. His deceived vision traps him into errors of fact, and huge errors of judgement.

He says, 'many of her friendships exploded into violent terminating quarrels'—(except for the cases of Roger Fry and Logan Pearsall Smith, I can think of no 'terminating quarrels'; and those began with the men)—'in the aftermath of which she could expect to see herself savagely caricatured in her late friend's next novel'; and he mentions *Crome Yellow*, and Lawrence's *Women in Love*.

He has exactly reversed chronology: the chill and, in the case of Lawrence, the long estrangement, were a consequence of the novel; there was no question, in either case, of the novel growing out of a quarrel. The story of both will be found in the present volume of the memoirs.

In fact, Ottoline does not appear in *Crome Yellow*.[1] What startled and hurt her was that most of her household and regular visitors were recognizable in uncharitable caricature.

There was never an entire breach over *Crome Yellow*. *Women in Love* led to complete estrangement, until she contracted the terrible disease in her jaw which, with the great probability of her death, shocked a number of people into reconciliation. After that she corresponded again with Lawrence. I must repeat, the estrangement was a consequence of the novel, not the novel of estrangement; and that what hurt Ottoline was that these novels should have been written by close and trusted friends.

There is another situation which, through his unawareness of Ottoline's true character, Mr. Holroyd has entirely misunderstood. When Dora Carrington was gradually abandoning Mark Gertler for Strachey, she was, he writes, 'certain . . . to attract the rancour of Ottoline who, much to Lytton's perplexity, showed the obverse of this rancour in a sudden flowering of her friendship with Gertler.' If Strachey was indeed perplexed, this revealed singular obtuseness of judgement in him.

---

[1] Aldous Huxley worked for a time, uncongenially, as a master at Eton. He was befriended there by Mrs. Warre Cornish, wife of the vice-provost. Her brother had married Anne, the novelist daughter of Thackeray. Mrs. Cornish was a woman of curious genius, famous for her inconsequential remarks. Her friendship must have been of great comfort to Huxley; yet, in his first book of fiction, *Limbo*, she appears entirely recognizable, but contemptuously caricatured. A short time after the publication of *Crome Yellow*, Ottoline happened to meet her. She said, 'When I next meet him I shall say "Mr. Huxley, I congratulate you on not putting your *hostess* into your novel"'.

Mr. Holroyd writes, 'Ottoline Morrell, indignant at the thought of losing Lytton to Carrington, whispered mischievous scandal in his ear.' Anybody who had but a small acquaintance with Ottoline would judge these implications to be, at least, beyond the probable.

In the first part of her memoirs, writing about her parties in Bedford Square, she tells in one place of her worried thoughts in the night: 'Had I introduced such a person to the other person they were suited for? . . . Had I neglected someone else?' And in another place she records, 'How I would torture myself afterwards as I went over the evening in my thoughts, thinking of someone I might have introduced to another and feeling that a lifelong friendship between these two might in consequence have come about.' She was far from being a breaker-up of partnerships; if she was not always wise when she concerned herself with the lives of other people, it was that she had, as her own reminiscences reveal, a propensity for match-making.

Strachey's settling down into what, for all the oddity of their relationship, was in effect a marriage, inevitably, as Ottoline wistfully records, placed a distance between him and many of his friends. But they were often meeting, and remained until the end of his life, as I can testify, on terms of affectionate intimacy. She did not, in fact, 'lose' Lytton to Carrington. A more probable interpretation of these events is not difficult to find.

There were in her life a number of men younger than her, to whom her relationship was maternal; Gertler, and the Spencer brothers, Stanley and Gilbert (especially the latter) were the most noticeable; I was the last. Ottoline would certainly have been distressed at *Gertler* losing Carrington to Lytton. It is quite likely that, being not over worldly-wise, she intervened in some way which Carrington greatly resented.[1] Once when I was at Ham Spray I said that I considered Ottoline a very remarkable woman. 'I don't think so!' snapped Carrington, 'not at all.' Unlike Strachey, when Duncan Grant and Vanessa Bell demurred at his praise of Ottoline, I did not conform. I dropped the subject. Yet Carrington's last contact with Ottoline revealed magnanimity.

[1] In the introduction to the first volume of these memoirs, on page 56, I told of a guest being fetched from Garsington by two friends. One was a young woman whom Ottoline had not seen for a long time and who distressed her by vehemently and coldly refusing to come into the house. The guest was Lytton Strachey; in the car were Ralph Partridge and Carrington. Since Partridge was alive when I wrote it, I did not identify these people.

In the short while she allowed herself between Strachey's death and her own, she contrived to thank Ottoline, who had brought them together, for being the cause of the greatest happiness she had known in her life.

Hans Andersen wrote an eerie story called *The Shadow*. A wise man becomes separated from his shadow, which returns to him in the form of a prosperous gentleman. As time goes by, the shadow becomes richer and the man poorer, until at last he is forced to hire himself to the shadow as—his shadow. The story ends with the shadow marrying a sovereign princess, and the man, who wishes to expose the shadow for what he is, being executed.

This is not a bad symbol for the history of Ottoline's reputation. Until her memoirs appeared, almost all that was publicly recorded about her came from the tales of Bloomsbury, and of their followers-on. Every fantasy, every false addition brought a further deviation until, when Mr. Holroyd set to work, he could find, not Ottoline but only the shadow. Yet the published letters to her from D. H. Lawrence and Katherine Mansfield ought to have suggested that something in the record had gone wrong. These letters, together with others from such men as Bertrand Russell, Aldous Huxley and Lytton Strachey, could not have been written to the puppet presented by Mr. Holroyd.

In conclusion, it may be pardonable to speculate a little as to why such wonderfully gifted writers as Virginia Woolf and Lytton Strachey could have written so maliciously and so treacherously about her (that their followers did the same is too sadly easy to understand). Her almost princely origin may have had, I suppose, something to do with it. They were comfortably yet ashamedly aware of her status; they enjoyed the friendship of a duke's sister, but to prove to themselves that they weren't snobs, they had to abuse her. And yet, I suspect there was something working deeper within them.

Not a great many years ago, one of the younger generation of Bloomsbury became, with entire sincerity, a Roman Catholic. Discussing this, one of the elders said he would rather she had become a fascist.[1] (My informant who heard this, himself an

---

[1] I can remember Lytton Strachey expressing to me horror at the concordat arranged between Mussolini and the Vatican. But he was not, as I surprisedly learned distressed at the countenance the papacy had thus given to the dictatorship: it was at the power gained by the church in such matters as education. The atheist in him was upset, not the liberal.

atheist of enthusiasm, thought it an exceedingly silly opinion.) They were all fanatical atheists, holding to their unfaith like the most bigoted of puritans. Ottoline, on the other hand, was, in all her being, although somewhat undenominational, an entirely religious creature.

In his *Books and Characters*, Lytton Strachey included an essay called 'The Rousseau Affair'. This ends with a panic-stricken attack by Diderot on Rousseau. 'May I never see that man again,' he wrote, 'he would make me believe in the devil and hell . . . you could hear those cries to the very end of my garden . . . poets would do well to put an immense distance between heaven and hell. In truth, my hand is trembling.' Strachey concludes, 'Diderot was writing from his heart. But he was wrong; the *"intervalle immense"*, across which, so strangely and so horribly, he had caught glimpses of what he had never seen before, was not the abyss between heaven and hell, but between the old world and the new.'

The abyss between Ottoline and these friends, though immense, was not so terrifying; many of them, and Strachey for certain, felt a warm and lasting affection for her. Yet, may it be that what confounded their judgement, what gave them a sort of vertigo, was that, from the world of material things, they were gazing uncomfortably at something they could not understand at all—a world of the spirit?

I must repeat here what I said at the beginning of this introduction. I have not been impelled only by the desire to defend Ottoline from attacks which I know to be wrong-headed. My intention has been to establish historical truth. Ottoline is now a public character, and thus a part of history. There are already people anxious to write about her; others will certainly follow. It is important that they should be able to estimate the value of evidence available to them. The few untruths I have dealt with are typical of many. From my treatment of them it will be seen, I trust, that, for evidence about Ottoline's character and actions, tales taken from Bloomsbury must be looked on with the doubt which a serious historian applies to old, unlikely and uncorroborated tradition.

PART I

CHAPTER I

Garsington at Last

At last on May 17th (1915) the day arrived for us to cross the threshold of our new home. Although we had been the owners of it for over two years, the old tenants remained in the house until the expiration of their lease. During that time it had seemed a far-away castle on a hill, towards which we were travelling, at first so dim and misty on the horizon that it didn't seem as if it ever would be a real house where we should actually live and sleep and talk.

By 1915 life in London had become entirely changed by the War. Politics and all our old interests had been swept away and there seemed no spot that one touched that didn't fly open and show some picture of suffering, some macabre dance of death. If one looked on a hoarding there was an appeal to men to 'join up', and go out to suffer. If one looked into an empty house, there were raw recruits sitting on bare benches, waiting to be drilled and sent out. If one just missed being run over, it was by some young Amazon, beautiful and ruthless, proud and happy to be dressed in khaki. In the constant procession of ambulances going to hospitals one saw tortured, maimed, human bodies lying. At least in the country there would be an escape from this, and probably interesting work to do on the farm and in the village.

The reason for which we had originally decided to leave London for the country was Julian's delicacy; it was essential for her health, so the doctors said, that she should not live in London. We arrived at Garsington on the eve of her ninth birthday. In my Journal I wrote:

'After nearly three years of waiting we have arrived here. I have dreaded it, dreaded the plunge of entering into such a completely new existence, and dreaded all the arranging and "house-moving", but now that it has actually happened, and that we are in the midst of it, not looking at it from a distance, over a hedge, I feel full of fresh hope, almost as if we had stepped out of a dark nightmare into a fresh magic world, where all is blossom and spring and tranquillity.'

Philip met me at the station when I arrived from Buxton, and as we climbed up the steep Garsington hill it seemed as if we were arriving at a village in the Apennines—the road so steep and so winding—but as we reached the top the sight of the fields of buttercups, the white and pink blossom against the old grey houses and the elms powdered with green leaves, drowsy cows munching their spring pasturage made it unmistakably England. And then suddenly the old church bells began to peal and peal and so continued all the evening. As Philip and I wandered round the garden after our tea, planning what to alter and what flowers to plant, I asked the gardener if this was the practice evening for the bellringers. He looked at me with shocked astonishment: 'Why! They are ringing to welcome you and Mr. Morrell.'

Next day Julian joined us. It was her ninth birthday. She had been staying for some years with one of Philip's sisters in their country house near Abingdon, to enable her to have country air and young companionship.

The house was still in great disorder, carpenters incessantly sawing and hammering, with deafening persistence; stonemasons running along boards with pails of mortar, joiners holding up window frames or door jambs for Philip's approval, repeated calls ringing through the house for Mr. Davis, the builder.

I left all the building and carpentry to Philip and devoted myself to the painting, and I had for my helper a charming, nervous, artistic fellow called Percy, who took endless trouble to get the exact green I wanted for one room, and the perfect but very elusive red I had set my heart on for the other. He would dash off on his bicycle to Oxford and return excited and flushed but triumphant with a tube of some precious 'Venetian Red' in his hand. 'Now, Percy, let us try again,' I in my holland overall, he in his white coat with his eternal cigarette hanging from his lip, would mix the little pots and dab and paint, and we would put our heads first on one side then on another to see if at last the magic ingredient had been found that made the old panelled room look as I could see it in my imagination, lined with real Venetian Red Lacquer. At last it looked beautiful and now only needed the panels to be outlined in gold, as I remembered them in the old panelled rooms at Bolsover. This I felt we could do ourselves. The green room never gave any trouble, but was lovely at once, a green that I have never seen equalled—it was so translucent that it gave one the impression of sea-green water flowing round us. (Alas! I hear our successors at Garsington have burnt off both these colours.) The long low hall was our next task. This we made lovely, pearly dove-grey, on which I painted a faint shade of pink that reflected the cardinal-red silk curtains. I had a winter sunset in my mind.

My maid and I had made all the curtains at home in London, and when the time came for hanging them there was endless running to and fro, and agitated discussions if a pair was found to be too short or too long. Tap, tap, tap, nailing the pelmets on the boards, and agonized excitement as to whether the yellow ones looked well in the green room, or the red ones perhaps in the hall. To answer all these questions Philip had to be called, fetched and consulted, as his taste was to my mind inevitable and perfect.

It was a very happy time, lovely fresh sunny May weather, the sound of birds in the garden floating in through the windows, and after the work, the still evenings in the garden. I realized that to get up early, put on an overall and plunge straight away after delicious coffee and toast into active life, running, fetching, carrying, painting and hammering, was a life of great happiness, peace and contentment; no engagements, no demands on one's inner life. I laughed to myself as I saw how easy and healthy practical work was—no wonder most women like it; no time for brooding, no time for puzzling over questions, for every question must be answered immediately.

When the painting was finished, the furniture from London arrived and had to be put into place. This was a dreadful task, for each piece of old furniture has such a definite character and mien of its own that if it doesn't like a room it is hopeless to induce it to look well or happy. It asserts itself and has to be moved elsewhere, however much it may inconvenience or disappoint. I wandered in and out of the rooms, planning and arranging, fetching and carrying. Percy continued his labours always with his cigarette. We had many talks about life and the War. I asked him if he was going to join up. 'I, my lady, not if I can help it. I never could abear the sight of a soldier.' But alas the time came when poor Percy had to go. Luckily he was taken prisoner, and although he had a bad time and suffered from the revolution in Germany, yet his nice, eccentric, kind English heart made him even as a prisoner beloved. His hair is white now, but when I see him, as I do occasionally, we paint over the red walls together in our memory and still sing the praises of the green room.

Here is an entry in my Journal:

'June 1st 1915. It has been lovely living this simple existence, isolated from the torrent of life, just concentrated on arranging and getting things straight in a small area, and there is always the daily excitement of adding something to the perfection of this lovely romantic place. It has magic and charm and feels curiously familiar, as if I had known it all my life. I love to sit in the garden under the great ilex tree and dream and plan what we can do here. There is much to do, for the garden is very rough. Philip has cleared the fishpond and restored its old oblong shape, putting back the stone coping, and then we hope in time to terrace the slope down from the house. It is already much more beautiful, we have made one terrace and a walk round the pond, and in the autumn we are arranging to plant yew hedges that will grow like a tall, dark wall round the water. It is more Italian than any other place in England that I have ever known—partly I suppose through being high on a hill and having a few dark cypresses already in the garden. I sit and wander about, when I am not busy in the house, and feel as if I were living in a dream, and as if life was hanging suspended, spellbound in a happy trance. Philip is away on the farm nearly all day, planting and sowing and preparing for cutting the hay. Julian is at lessons or scampering about with her young Swiss governess; whom I have just engaged—Mademoiselle Juliette Baillot.[1] She is very young and pretty and simple, and rather naïve, but is perfect for Julian as a companion, and they seem very happy together.

'I dread anyone coming and spoiling, breaking, this lovely spellbound existence, but yet I feel it is selfish to enjoy it all alone—the garden is full of flowers and the trees are just in leaf now. I have promised the Lawrences and the Cannans and Gertler and his friends that they shall come. Letters arrive from Lawrence impatient to be here. Yes, I must rouse myself out of this peace and wake up to real life again, and then I shall have to

[1] She came as governess and companion to Julian. She was to marry Sir Julian Huxley. I remember her as a singularly beautiful young woman.

hear voices and controversy and arguments, and war will break through the misty dream screen. I have kept it at bay for the last few weeks here, but if once I let my mind go back to it, all peace and happiness will be gone; for thoughts and ideas are swept away by the ghastly fact of mental and bodily pain. The destructive torrent is so strong that it sweeps everyone with it, and even if one could stand aside and cultivate one's garden I should feel it frivolous and heartless. Any delicate creative effort is blasted and seems trivial, for the War is so real and terrible, it blots out anything else, and makes any other work seem valueless, except that of passionate resistance, and that at times seems quixotic and futile.

'But I should like to make this place into a harbour, a refuge in the storm, where those who haven't been swept away could come and renew themselves and go forth strengthened. But people are very difficult to manage. The young Cambridge men are so critical and superior and disdainful, and lift up their hands in horror at men like D. H. Lawrence who have fire and genius. They tolerate Bertie because he was at Cambridge and is of course intensely intellectual. I feel despondent about it all. People are so rigid, and only like to move in little circles on little toy railway lines surrounded by their admirers, they don't want to venture forth, and are afraid of possible persecution.

'But now I will bestir myself and ask some people here and have a party for my birthday. I will ask the Cannans and Lawrences and Bertie and Maria[1] will be here. Bertie and Lawrence can make friends and plan a "revolution" and a "New World", and write manifestos together. And as it is my birthday and lovely summer, they will have to be nice and kind to each other, and not rage and quarrel.

'I have had some nice letters from D. H. Lawrence lately.'

---

[1] Maria Nys, who was to marry Aldous Huxley.

CHAPTER II

A Birthday Party. Decorating the House.
The Rainbow and D. H. Lawrence

On June 15th I find the following entry in my Journal:

'The birthday party arrived. The house, of course, was very unfinished, but I did my best to make them comfortable, and Lawrence was charming and sympathetic and interested in all that we are doing here. He helped us decorate with gold the panels in the red room. We were an odd looking company, tall and short, thin and thick, dressed in white overalls, egg-cups of gold paint in our hands, creeping slowly round the room, outlining each panel with a fine paint-brush. Someone had to climb up on to the steps to do the beams, and poor Bertie was sent up and nearly expired from the heat, but it was all fun and Lawrence of course did his far quicker and straighter than any of us. Frieda sat on the table in the middle of the room, swinging her legs and laughing and mocking at us, giving advice as to what curtains she would have. She has a terrible irritant quality, and enjoys tormenting, and she liked to taunt me because I was taking trouble to make the house nice. Of course to her, who hadn't a home, and who carries her belongings round the world in a few trunks, it seems absurd to spend time and trouble on making a house really nice, although when Philip offered to adapt the old "monastic building" here into a house for them she required so much done that it would have cost far more than we could afford. It was an anxious visit for with Frieda one feels one is sitting with a tigress who will spring and rend either Lawrence or one of us at any moment. She was jealous that we all liked and admired Lawrence, or Lorenzo[1] as she calls him, and that we did not consider her as important a person as he is. She even said in a loud, challenging voice, "I am

---

[1] Ottoline told me how, when they were quarrelling, she would sometimes draw herself up and say, 'Do not forget, Lorenzo, I am a baroness!'

just as remarkable and important as Lorenzo." Indeed, in all our talks she was very aggressive and self-assertive. I began to fear she would make it difficult to be friends with him, she was already turning him against Bertie because Bertie didn't flatter her. She has educated herself on Nietzsche; she appears to be a woman that Strindberg might have married and hated, and is what is called a "clever fool". Naïvely, I did not realize that the Lawrences were not happy here, but apparently she became jealous and they had a miserable time together, fighting and quarrelling all night. He came down on the morning of their last day looking whipped, forlorn and crestfallen, and she went off in a high temper to London. I shall always see that unhappy, distraught, pathetic figure standing in the hall hesitating whether he should remain here or whether he should follow her to London. Philip strongly urged him to assert himself and leave her. Of course he didn't, but meekly followed her to London. I retired from the controversy for I felt certain that he was too bound up with her ever to leave her. He is very weak with her, although he abuses her to us and indeed often to her face he shouts abusive things, yet she will always win if she wants to; for she had ten times the physical vitality and force that he has, and always really dominates him, however much he may rebel and complain. He is by tradition and instinct faithful to a wife, and far too timid and sensitive to face life alone, for although he has the flaming ideas of a propagandist he has neither knowledge of the world nor the calm assurance that carries conviction. He soon becomes disappointed, angry, fierce and intolerant at not being attended to, and after a frenzy of angry barks he turns with a drooping tail and seeks refuge in Frieda, his "dark abode".

'How odd the effect two human beings can have on each other. Two ingredients separate may be good and balanced but mixed together beget havoc and discord. I always remember these lines of Browning:

> *Once I saw a chemist take a pinch of powder,*
> *Simple dust it seemed—and half unstop a phial.*
> *Out dropped harmless dew. "Mixed nothings make," quoth he,*
> *"Something." So they did. A thunderclap but louder,*
> *Lightning flash, but fiercer, put spectators' nerves to trial.*
> *Sure enough we learnt what was, imagined what might be!*

'Frieda and Lawrence mixed certainly put spectators' nerves to trial, and it is easy to imagine what might be! How well the soothsayer warned Antony beware of Caesar:

> *Stay not by his side.*
> *Thy Demon—that's thy spirit which keeps thee—is*
> *Noble, courageous, high, unmatchable,*
> *Where Caesar's is not. But near him thy angel*
> *Becomes a fear, as being o'erpower'd—therefore*
> *Make space enough between you.*

'Poor Lawrence, what a distraught creature he is underneath; the constant friction and fighting with Frieda will wear his nerves out in time. I fear he will have to kill all his gentle tender side, so as to have peace with her, and in time he will adapt himself more and more to her, although subconsciously he will resent it. But he will never part from her, he is too moral, and is bound to her by some need of his nature.'

After they had gone, Frieda in a rage with me and with everybody and Lawrence crushed and unhappy, but following her like a whipped dog, I thought I should never see them again. She accused me, I found out afterwards, of having ignored and slighted her and of having a 'soul mush' with Lawrence. I thought he would never dare speak to us again, but I was to learn that such scenes did not have the permanent effect on them that they would have on most people. With the Lawrences they are like violent mountain storms that rage with thunder and lightning and then pass, and in a few hours the sky is calm, serene and sunny, for a brief spell at least. I wrote to him about *The Rainbow* when it came out, and told him that I thought the second half was very fine, and as he had had no praise for it my letter was welcome and made the sun to shine. He had the belief that he could, as with a wave of his hand bring a revolution to pass in England, and that his friends were but poor, craven laggards who were too lazy and unbelieving to bestir themselves, but the failure of *The Rainbow* made him realize that at this time there were no ears open to him. *The Rainbow* was suppressed as immoral. Philip did all he could in the House of Commons to get the ban removed, but without success. We lent our copy to Sir John Simon and other influential men, who read it with eyes that greedily swept the pages for indecent passages. The suppression of this book was a great blow to poor Lawrence. It had been a long piece of work into which he had put all his energies, and he was at the moment very hard up. The suppression was due to a hysterical newspaper review by James Douglas[1] in a Sunday paper. In my Journal I find:

'I went up to London for the day and went to see the Lawrences at Hampstead, in the little house which they have taken. Frieda was awkward and rather shyly aggressive and ashamed like a child, but I ignored it and was friendly to her. We had a long talk and went a walk on the Heath. Lawrence said he must leave England, and go to a country that has a future before it, a country that is in the spring of its life. Here in England the autumn had set in, life is dead, the land dead, the people are dead sapless sticks. He feels he must leave before he goes dead too. He is determined to go off to America and write for Americans. I think he may be right to go, although I think his judgement is all wrong about England. Of course while the War goes on everything is horrible. But he may be right to go for himself. Youth, genius, has an instinct perhaps to save itself, to protect itself from the depression and contagion of death; and it will be better for him to go to fresh fields than to stay here bemoaning and wailing the decay of England, especially as his health is very bad, and there is the complication of Frieda being aggressively German.

'Lawrence has a passion to preach, to dominate. His preaching, I fear, is too remote from what men need now. He is too isolated, too remote from the trend of thought of those that he would sway and influence. He really is not a practical leader although very inspiring and stimulating to individuals who understand him and who are anxious to learn from him. Just now he is very excited about two young men that he has met; he thinks they will do great things; to hear him talk of them, one would imagine the future of England is in their hands. One is a poet who has been at the War and is now in hospital and whose nerves are very bad, Bob Nichols, and the other is a musician, Philip Heseltine.[2] He says that I *must* know them. He is determined that we should all go out and join him in Florida and make a com-

---

[1] A journalist who made a point of attacking what he believed to be dangerously immoral books. He was the prime cause of Radcliffe Hall's *The Well of Loneliness* being suppressed. He declared that he would rather give strychnine to a young person than this book. 'Strychnine,' he added, 'kills bodies. This book will kill souls.'

[2] Better known by his pseudonym, Peter Warlock.

munity there, or perhaps on an island in the Pacific. It doesn't attract me at all! I certainly see no reason to leave England. And I feel one ought to remain and put all one's energies into helping on things here. Lawrence is too impatient, he has not got the political instinct, which means that one must have endless patience, tolerance and wisdom. He is far too reckless and rapid in denunciation, and Frieda urges him on in his intolerant denunciations, and so he rushes about with one idea after another like an excited dog, barking and barking at an imaginary enemy, but he cannot put forward any solid ideas, and mere denunciations do no good.'

CHAPTER III

Two Artists and the C. P. Sangers. A Flat for Bertie Russell

'Well, that's over!' I said to myself as I waved the last of that birthday party off. 'It began very merrily, but when Frieda is about I suppose it is pretty certain that some storm will arise. Her egotism and vitality together make an electric turmoil, and she is entirely careless as to what happens around her, what lives, hearts, cups or chairs are broken, as long as she can indulge her pastime of asserting her own importance by buffeting any unfortunate being that she imagines doesn't bow down before her. Poor Lawrence, how dreadful to be tied to her as he is by his need of some strong big woman. And how humiliating to have to follow her, like a whipped dog, even if he does manage sometimes to get in a snap and snarl!'

But the beauty and the freshness of this summer are still undefiled by Frieda and Lawrence and their foolish self-assertions.

The Japanese dancer Ito was the next visitor. This quiet little figure who seemed as if he had emerged out of an old Japanese print put himself back into one here. For he spent his days fishing in one of the ponds under blossoming quince and apple trees, while Maria Nys in a white dress flitted round about him with adoring eyes.

The next to come was Guevara, the Chilian painter, with Duncan Grant. I hadn't realized that Guevara's mind was entirely absorbed, not with his pictorial art, which I admired very much, but with the art of boxing; he could think and talk of nothing else. His thick voice would maunder on all day talking of 'boxthing', and of his own prowess, which was purely illusory as he was, I heard, hopelessly bad. He even begged me to send for someone from Oxford to come and 'boxthe' with him on the lawn, which I entirely declined to do.

The next group to enter the tall gates were a more solemn little company—Dora and Charles Sanger, Mrs. Hamilton and

Harry Norton.[1] Charlie Sanger was like a very clever, alert, shy, nervous bird, his thin body in a white waistcoat tilted forward, and his head looking up, *pince-nez* on nose attached with a black cord, greeting us with a shy quick talk and a nervous laugh; Dora, red-faced, untidy, blowzy, unkempt and rather lame and clumsy, with quick furtive black eyes, looking at everything to see how luxurious and self-indulgent we were, but eating so greedily, scones, cakes and jam and butter at tea that my house-keeping mind was aghast, wondering in those days of rationing how to provide butter and jam for tea on Sunday, if so much disappeared at Saturday's tea. Dora had obviously starved herself for the benefit of the poor for many weeks past, and was now enjoying a good tea on her own account. Mrs. Hamilton and Harry Norton came with them. Mrs. Hamilton we had got to know, I think, through pacifist work. She wrote novels, was cheerful, vigorous, free, independent and rather boy-like; her husband had vanished and she lived alone in the Adelphi. She was very competent and right-minded in her political views. All this time we saw a good deal of her as she worked hard in London and was glad to come down to us for week-ends to have a change and rest and good company. She made friends with Bertie Russell and our other political friends. I liked her but found her loud, clear, insistent voice very trying. She has passed out of our life now. I don't know exactly why—simply I think because she is really only interested in Labour politics, and our interests have developed in other directions. She was for a time a Labour M.P. and a devoted friend of Ramsay MacDonald, and has written his life.

Harry Norton we had known for some years. He was a Fellow of Trinity Cambridge and a brilliant mathematician and had apparently a very remarkable future before him—but unfortunately he became a hypochondriac, and now is a recluse.

This Sunday Charlie Sanger and Mrs. Hamilton sat on the lawn and talked endlessly of international diplomacy. Charlie's talk was rapid, sometimes witty, and concise; sometimes Norton, when not ruminating on his own health, would contribute a very pointed remark, revealing what a good mind he had, hidden

[1] Mrs. Hamilton was a worker in the Labour Party, and a friend of Ramsay MacDonald. Harry Norton, a Cambridge mathematician, was a friend of Lytton Strachey—and, indeed, of all that group. Each is mentioned briefly in the first volume.

under his egotistical gloom and lethargy. Dora and I enjoyed the sun and the garden and wandered over the fields of buttercups and gossiped and talked of poetry and lamented the War and the tragedy of the derelict and interned Germans. She was extremely generous and kind to them—indeed to anyone who was down and out. Forgetful and negligent of her own person and of her husband's comfort, she would devote herself to anyone who claimed her sympathy.

At this time Philip had arranged a very comfortable flat at the Bailiff's House for Bertie Russell, and I furnished it and made it very comfortable. There was a charming room for him to work in, with a marvellous view across to the Berkshire Downs; he arrived and settled in with his books and started his work. Whenever we had visitors that he liked he would come over and have his meals with us. In my Journal I find:

'Bertie arrived yesterday and is settled in his rooms. I made them gay and pretty with flowers. He is gloomy and sceptical about everything, and about his own work, but it is really very good—a set of lectures on the New State; *Social Reconstruction* they are to be called. His brain seems to be working well, indeed very brilliantly. He said yesterday on our walk together, "I find it difficult to talk to the ordinary mortal, for the language they use is so inaccurate that to me it seems absurd. The ordinary view of life is too immature to be tolerable to me. When I talk to an ordinary person I feel I am talking baby language, and it makes me very lonely." Oh dear, how terrible to be so removed from human life. He went on to discuss his lectures and his view of truth, comparing it with Lawrence's view of truth—his own, of course, is scientific truth, provable by mathematics and physics, Lawrence's is a subjective truth, something which is *felt* to be true, as an inward conviction that such a picture or a view is beautiful.

'There really seem to me three worlds—the one which Bertie calls the *real* world, the world of the scientist, which is after all queer and eccentric enough when one knows it; then the world of the ordinary businessman, stocks and shares, money-turnover, organization of trade; and then the world of art, poetry and of feeling, of spiritual perceptions and imaginative creation and fantasy, which I suppose depends on the other worlds, and which picks and chooses and absorbs what is necessary to feed and enrich its life. This is the world that Shakespeare gave us, human life permeated with a rich glow and vitality from the affections, the senses, the imagination. This is my world. Bertie really enjoys it in literature, but he never treats it seriously; he looks on it simply as an opiate to dull the pain of living; he never seems to contemplate the possibility that it could be a Utopia, absorbing into itself the other worlds as they are developed, cleared and purified, and made fit to take their place in this ordered and yet fluid and ever-growing existence.'

CHAPTER IV

Henry and Charles Bentinck in Gallipoli. Lytton Writes Eminent Victorians. Bishop Gore Goes Harvesting

On July 17th 1915 I find I wrote:

'Julian and I went into Oxford yesterday to Mrs. Morrell's fête at Black Hall. There were crowds of Oxford people there. I found I disliked them violently—their ideas so stupid, so conventional and cruel and inhuman. They are filled with hatred to the Germans or to anyone else who is not extremely warlike. I felt like a white moth amongst them all. The little Catholic children's dancing though was lovely, they danced a ballet taught to them by an old nun. What was her past, I wonder? She was the only nice, sympathetic person there. One could see that she still vibrated to the rhythm of the music, and that underneath her voluminous black cloth habit her limbs still danced the old steps. She seemed very happy. Philip came down from London and picked me up, and we all drove back together. Such a relief to get away. The sunset was lovely, it cast a wonderful pink light on the cream-coloured road as we drove home. It is one of the things that always gives me great joy, and such things creep into one's heart and are great treasures, unspoilt, and unknown to anyone.'

A few days later:

'Bertie and I had a walk in the rain yesterday. He gets dreadfully on my nerves, he is so stiff, so self-absorbed, so harsh and unbending in mind or body, that I can hardly look at him, but have to control myself and look away. And of course he feels this, and it makes him harsher and more snappy and crushing to me. What can I do? I feel I *must* be alone and go my own way to develop my life, my own internal life. Bertie crushes it out; he would remake me; and the effort of resisting him and of protecting myself makes me desperate. It is far better to be alone than to be false. I am too stupid to be in touch with pure

45

intellectuals and too clearheaded to be in touch with the mediocre.'
  Later I find:
'I have been very anxious for many months about Henry
(my brother) at the Dardanelles. Charlie is there too but somehow he is more suited to it, as he is a soldier by profession. Henry
got dysentery and nearly died, but he is at home now, which is
an immense relief. Birdie[1] looks a wreck from anxiety and
hysterical emotion, poor thing. I went up to London to see
Henry—he is very depressed and showed no sign of pleasure at
seeing me, which disappointed me but I feel he has seen such
horrors that it has taken all the life and spirit out of him. Charlie
is still out there; he has been wounded once and has gone back
again to fight. I don't think he feels it as much as Henry. They
both think it hopeless to get through at the Dardanelles. It has
all been a miserable waste of life and money. The loss of life there
is ghastly, about 1,000 a day fall ill with dysentery. Philip had a
long interesting letter from Jos. Wedgwood who is there; the
description he gives of the landing is unbelievably ghastly, the
sea red with the blood of the wounded and killed. Henry told
me that it was very moving hearing his men in the Derbyshire
Yeomanry talking at night in the trenches—men from Lan-
cashire, Derbyshire, miners from Durham and Nottinghamshire
and far north Northumberland, all speaking in their different
dialects of their homes and of life in England, crouched there in
muddy, oriental dugouts. His devoted manservant, Brown, had
joined up and was in the regiment. I heard that he would creep
along the trench every night and ask Henry "Is there anything
more I can do for your lordship tonight?" He would ask this as
if he had just laid out Henry's evening dress clothes.'
  In August I find this entry:
'We have had many, many people here. It seems to me crowds
come and go, the house full every week-end, and overflowing
into the Bailiff's House. In July Vanessa Bell and Duncan Grant
came and Lytton Strachey, who stayed on some time and indeed
has spent most of this summer here, coming and going as he
wished, lying out on the lawn or writing in a quiet room his
book on *Eminent Victorians*. He has been very gay and delightful,
full of *bonne humeur* because he is working hard and his writing
is going well. He is an adorable companion. He reads aloud to
us in the evenings or on wet afternoons. The other day he read

[1] Lady Henry Bentinck.

46

me the whole of Dryden's *All for Love*. We sat together a whole afternoon rocked with emotion and enjoyment of it. Another day he read me passages from Racine's *Phèdre* and *Andromaque*—he reads them in a voice that might be Sarah Bernhardt's. It is almost upsetting hearing this female hysterical screaming voice coming from a man with a long beard! But he reads with incomparable accent and squeezes the utmost value and meaning from his subject. Another evening, when Bertie came over, he read us a chapter which he had just finished from his book, *Eminent Victorians*. I have grown very fond of him, and we have become much more intimate—he seems happier now (Henry Lamb is only a shadow in the past), and he makes friends with the young people who come here for the week-end. He is a wonderfully sympathetic friend and his rectitude of mind is enchanting. His health is very poor, and he suffers a great deal from dyspepsia. He has to have very simple food. I hear in the village he is called sometimes "Christ", sometimes "Judas", on account of his long beard.'

Later on I find another entry:

'Philip is continually up and down to London for the House of Commons, working hard for conscientious objectors. During the harvest I worked in the fields, "shocking" and helping in the rick building. I enjoyed it immensely. It is lovely standing on top of a rick as it grows up and up beneath one, and the old men working so rhythmically amid a continual chime of jokes going around. They get hold of one joke and it ripples around and round until it is quite worn out. I tried to get Bertie to come and help; he came one day but it was clear that he was hopelessly bored to death—his face drawn out to its full length—and longed to get away. I cannot understand not imbibing some of the pleasure that comes to one as one works at this antique labour of storing the grain. These hot glowing August evenings, when the men work with ardour to get done before rain comes, make one happy and excited. How I love to see old Trinder (the carter) pitchforking the sheaves on to the long waggon as if he was lifting a bundle of feathers. It is sad for Bertie not to possess any of these simple vital instincts, they give one very comforting contact with life and relieve the tension of pure intellect. He only feels life through his brain, or through sex, and there is a gulf between these two separate departments. It is this that maddens and annoys Lawrence so much in him.'

While the harvest was on, the Bishop of Oxford, Charles Gore, came over from Cuddesdon to tea, and insisted on coming down to the fields and helping us gather up the sheaves. He said he was quite accustomed to 'shocking', in every sense of the word. He was a dear man, very witty, humorous, fastidious, intellectual, an artist in thought and feeling, and in spirit a saint. I was rather shy with him, for he was always more at ease with men than women, but during the years that he lived at Cuddesdon he was the only neighbour that we cared to see. He would walk across the fields to tea, and I think he enjoyed coming and meeting men like Lytton Strachey and Bertie Russell, and later John Middleton Murry. Philip and I would often walk back with him and have good talks. He gave up his bishopric on July 1st 1919. I will find the little note he wrote me then. As I think of him now he is one of the men that I feel was nearer perfection than any I have known, free from selfishness and with an aristocratic spontaneity and courage, but humility before God. I imagine very solitary in his inner life. He often spoke of having always been 'outside the herd', even at school.

I was rather amused to hear, many years after this, that an old lady living in a large house nearby had remonstrated with Gore about coming to see me so often. 'Did not he think it might be very unwise?'

Gore's answer was, 'Oh, but I like her so much and she amuses me!'

CHAPTER V

The Friends Who Shared Our Life

What a huge party we were in those days, sitting tightly packed together round the long table in the red room for breakfast, lunch, tea and dinner. How did we ever house such a company and feed them in those lean war days? I cannot now tell. They all used to rush in on a Friday or Saturday, some by motor bikes, some by train, and crowd round the table, and then clamour for towels and bathing suits large and small, and run down to bathe in the old fish pond, and afterwards sit or lie on the lawn endlessly talking, talking. And then in the evening play games, act charades or dance until I thought the old oak floor would fall through. With the exception of Lytton, most of them were all young, full of vitality and indignation against the War. They had seemed a relief in London from the warlike people and it seemed good to gather round us young and enthusiastic pacifists. I didn't find that there was anyone that I was specially drawn to or desired to be intimate with but still I was interested in them all, and threw myself into their lives, and their affairs of all sorts.

It was always a great happiness when Lytton was with us, for I felt intimate with him, and we shared the excitements and interests that were wafted through each day. He was always very sympathetic to me and witty. I wrote of him at the time as '*digne*, fantastic, witty, sympathetic, political, passionate and excited, but too purely English not to be irritated by my flights and frenzies, as he calls them. *Au fond* he is rigidly classic, and hates and mistrusts wildness or religion—the things after all which I love best.'

He was always absurdly English, and even his food must be as solid and English as possible; his notion of a perfect meal being roast beef and vegetables at Simpsons in the Strand. But then he had long generations of well-to-do, cultivated, intellectual, upper middle-class English ancestors behind him, and was proud to

49

remember that a Strachey is mentioned in one of Shakespeare's historical plays. He looked very tall, thin and intellectual, among the crowd of unpolished young people that came—he still wore his hair long like Augustus John, but he had discarded his ear-rings, and very soon cut his hair and wore a collar, partly perhaps for his own security, for in those times of intolerance and suspicion any eccentricity was liable to attract persecution as a foreigner and a spy.

Another figure that came and went was Maynard Keynes. Somehow he was always associated with Lytton, they were at Cambridge together and were then great friends, although at times rivals for the affections of some young friend. I liked Keynes immensely, and he has always been particularly kind to me. After an operation for appendicitis, we asked him to come and he spent some time in the summer with us, convalescing, and during those days lying out on the lawn I got to know him well. I find I wrote of him as 'that satyr Keynes, greedy of work, fame, influence, domination, admiration; *soigné* and attractive, and desirous of being attractive, very sympathetic to the am-bitions of young men. His influence and his advice are always in favour of hard work, and point towards the high road of life, not to flights and dilettantisms. His intellect is of a fine steel-like quality, and his mind works more rapidly than any I have ever known—even Bertie, who obviously doesn't like him very much, acknowledges that he thinks far quicker than he does himself, and that he can manipulate complicated abstract and economic subjects with the greatest ease. But his manner except to a few intimate friends is dominating and borders on the insolent.'

This seems to me now, years later, fairly accurate, but these scrappy sentences do not give the atmosphere of his personality—a detached, meditating and yet half-caressing interest in those he is speaking to, head on one side, a kindly tolerant smile and very charming eyes wandering, searching and speculating, then probably a frank, intimate and perhaps laughing home-thrust, which may or may not illuminate one's own self-knowledge.

Very soon after this time he was called from Cambridge to act as financial adviser to the Treasury. Bertie Russell met him one day at Cambridge running round to borrow a motor bicycle. 'What *do* you want that for?' Bertie asked him. 'To get to London.' 'Won't the train do?' 'No, they have sent for me to come to the Treasury immediately.' And at the Treasury he remained until after Versailles, endeavouring with all his wisdom and cunning to steer things aright, and he was one of the very few influential men at the Conference who had the decency to consult the German delegates. But of this he has himself written in *The Economic Consequences of the Peace*.

Maynard was still devoted to Duncan (Grant), who seems to flit to and fro like a winged elf, sympathetic and charming in body and in heart, looking on the world through his wide pale eyes. What he sees is a vision all his own, a lovely coloured vision of fantasy and humour and which sometimes embalms this old world with an alchemy of his own. His hand when he paints seems guided by a magic impulse that fills it with a lyrical harmony of colour and form, making it sing with beauty. Perhaps he is as a painter what Virginia Woolf is as a writer. He and Vanessa Bell (Virginia's sister) have lived together since about 1915. She is devoted to him—and, I have always felt, very possessive of him, but no one could ever 'possess' Duncan. They are, however, very much married, although she seems to me much older than he is—for he had the rare secret of eternal youth. Vanessa is beautiful as a Watts painting or a William Morris drawing. Her character seems to me like a broad river, not worried or sensitive to passers-by. She carries along the few barques that float with her on her stream of life, her two sons and daughter, but the sea towards which she flows is her painting, above all the thing that is of importance to her.

Devoted to her, but perhaps even more to Duncan, was David ('Bunny') Garnett—an odd rather loutish figure with a habit, which had perhaps been formed by peering into microscopes, of waggling his head and poking it towards one, and staring very intently into one's face without any expression on his own countenance. What he thinks of when he does this I could never tell, but he expresses himself to most people by almost excessive affection—he will kiss anybody, male or female, murmuring 'You are a darling'. Whether this is a sign of an overflowing affectionate heart I don't know, or simply a habit to save himself the trouble of talking. His face remains quite expressionless. He was at this time studying biology and botany, and he seemed to me a mixture of scientific interest and of his mother's Tolstoyan Russian peasant sympathies, upon which was spread a veneer of Bloomsbury culture.

Then there was Clive Bell, who was the faithful 'hanger on'

attached to this group, and who had the momentary charm of the flatterer. He is the sipper, the taster, the professional connoisseur of life, which is easy to him, for he is without depth or passion. His sensuality, of which he is so proud, is stimulated almost entirely by vanity. If these characteristics were those of a graceful young Adonis they would have a certain gay, youthful charm, but already Clive was rather podgy, his ginger-tinted hair is thinning, and his abdomen protruding, and he seemed even then to appear more as a balloon than a Prince Charming!

Then there was Mark Gertler and Gilbert Cannan. Both Mark and his friend Carrington, a Slade School student, came very often to Garsington. She was attractive as a wild shaggy Exmoor pony is attractive. Mark had been deeply and tragically in love with her for some years. She neither wholly responded nor wholly rejected him. They used to meet almost daily and she seemed to enjoy his company and vitality, his good and amusing talk and his devotion. One felt they would inevitably sooner or later marry, as they were so bound up with each other. She had a fat lumpy face, a mop of fair sunburnt hair, elusive wandering blue eyes which rarely looked at one, except when she wished to captivate, and then she would look up like a child, with an odd uncertain rather furtive smile. Her figure was active and sturdy, dressed in the Augustus John fashion of tight bodice and full skirt. She seemed at this time very unsure of herself, and although she was apparently very frank, I felt that she was really excessively timid and afraid of being sincere.

Attached to these two, and devoted to them both was Brett— also a Slade School student. She was a daughter of Lord Esher, with something of his talent but rather more eccentric. She had detached herself from the worldly milieu of her home, and had not yet found many friends except Gertler and Carrington. She was a slim, pretty young woman, looking much younger than she really was. She had a Joe Chamberlain nose, a peach-like complexion, rather a rabbit mouth and no chin. She was of the squirrel type and, poor thing, was very deaf. I liked her and felt so sorry for her, as her deafness made it difficult for her to be friends with people, and I knew her family were not very kind or sympathetic to her. I felt she was a sort of Cinderella, and that I had to help her to find new friends, and have her stay with us as much as possible.

The one old friend who came was Augustine Birrell. I first

met him before I married, at the time I was planning to live in Bedford Square with Hilda Douglas-Pennant. He was amused, interested and pleased that anyone so young as I then was should want to live in that old-fashioned quarter of London, and his whimsical humour played with thoughts of my future career. Perhaps too he was surprised at my love of literature. He promised to visit me at No. 29 Bedford Square, but the visit had to be postponed, as very soon I became engaged to Philip and we went to live in Grosvenor Road. The magnetism of Bedford Square still held me and we soon left Grosvenor Road and came to that lovely quarter. Augustine Birrell and his wife constantly came to dine with us. Now after her death he liked to come and pace the lawn at Garsington, or to sit in a long chair under the ilex, talking to Lytton Strachey or Maynard Keynes, and even, wrapped in one of my black Italian capes, looking like a Napoleonic general, going down to the pond for a swim. He looked very handsome with his fine head and thick grey hair, and sensitive humorous face, with a look of Thackeray and a flavour of the wit and wisdom of Doctor Johnson in his talk. He was genial and kind and interested in the young, and they all liked him and enjoyed his kind-hearted cynicism.

On Sundays Violet Asquith and her father, the Prime Minister, would often come over, sometimes bringing some friends with them, treating us, as I laughingly said at the time, as a convenient and entertaining 'side-show' for their guests. He never seemed depressed, or worried by the War, but remained the same genial self-indulgent old man, interested in everything that he found to hand, especially in Julian's lessons, and in a little girl called Lalage who was then living with us as a companion for Julian. I had always an affection for the old man, and was grateful to him for all he had done for me before I married, but I never thought he had much heart, only sentimental emotion. Already at this time he seemed to have lost the austerity that had held his rather lazy easy-going pleasure-loving temperament in shape. I often remembered that in the old days, when I saw more of him, he pointed out to me the Collect for Easter Eve.[1] As I looked up at him in surprise that this one should have appealed to him, he

---

[1] 'Grant, O Lord, that we are baptized into the death of thy blessed Son our Saviour Jesus Christ, so by continually mortifying our corrupt affections we may be buried with them; and that through the grave and gate of death, we may pass to our joyful resurrection . . .'

said, 'You don't know how much I need that prayer.' His brain remained a good instrument, but it seemed to be an instrument that didn't move or develop, fire and sensibility were dimmed, and the way of life that prevailed at his home altered his values, and made it easy for him to reconcile himself to the War, and indeed passively to accept without any struggle or indignant horror the wrecking of Europe, and the overthrow of all the old Liberal principles and party.

CHAPTER VI

D. H. Lawrence Speaks

During all these months I was seeing a great deal of Bertie and hearing from Lawrence, and was a witness of the strange almost passionate friendship that had sprung up between them since the day I had taken Bertie down to Pulborough to meet Lawrence. At first I hoped that they could work together, as they seemed really to like each other and Bertie had a great admiration for the fiery prophet. He thought of him as a second Ezekiel, and had a belief in his vision. But it was impossible that such a friendship should last. Bertie found Lawrence too wild, too intellectually undisciplined, and Bertie seemed rigid to Lawrence, who always grew impatient with anyone who was not pliant to his domination. He very soon felt baffled by Bertie's indomitable intellect, his reserve, his self-control. It angered him that a man whose views were so sympathetic to his own, and who, he saw, had so much passionate force, should be apparently so dominated by his intellect. He threw himself against Bertie like a wave dashing itself against a rock, he believed that he could make him more human, more optimistic, not so encased in his hard steel-like intellect. And, too, Bertie's ingrained habit of pessimism, and his concentrated passionate suffering annoyed Lawrence. But here Lawrence's habitual impatience did not let him see far enough into Bertie's character, also perhaps a tinge of envy coloured his judgement. He said that Bertie suffered, not because he knew too much of life, but from having 'experienced too little'. Lawrence was mistaken. Bertie was not so ignorant of life, nor was he detached, but his exact mind demanded too logical a world, his mathematical instinct found in the jumble of life a chaos that he despaired of putting in order. His passion for the beauty of perfection, mathematical exactitude, made him view this fluid tossing life with angry and tragic impatience, and he certainly was prone to see evil in a day's walk rather than good. But for some time Bertie kept up with Lawrence and even had him to stay with him at Cambridge, and these letters which came from Lawrence and Bertie at this time tell of some of their impressions:

(*1915*)   *Monday mg.*

Lawrence is gone, disgusted with Cambridge, but not with me, I think. I felt that we got on *very* well with each other, and made real progress towards intimacy. His intuitive perceptiveness is *wonderful*—it leaves me gasping in admiration.

Keynes came to dinner, and we had an interesting but rather dreadful evening. Keynes was hard, intellectual, insincere— using intellect to hide the torment and discord in his soul. We pressed him hard about his purpose in life—he spoke as tho' he only wanted a succession of agreeable moments, which of course is not really true. Lawrence likes him but can't get on with him; I get on with him, but dislike him. Lawrence has the same feeling against sodomy as I have; you had nearly made me believe there is no great harm in it, but I have reverted; and all the examples I know confirm me in thinking it sterilizing.

Lawrence is wonderfully lovable. The mainspring of his life is love—the universal mystical love—which inspires even his most vehement and passionate hate. It is odd that his *thinking* is coloured by Self—he imagines men more like him than they are. I think his thinking is quite honest, but there are painful things it hasn't realized.

(*Cambridge*) *1915*   *Sunday evg.*

I gave your letter to Lawrence who says he will come to tea with you tomorrow. I don't think he will get on with Goldie[1]— he hates everybody here, as was to be expected. I was grateful to you for telling me Keynes was up—I am having him to dinner tonight. Lawrence had rather liked him before—but seeing him this morning at 11, in pyjamas, just awake, he felt him corrupt and unclean. Lawrence has quick sensitive impressions which I don't understand, tho' they would seem quite natural to you. They are marvellous. I love him more and more. I couldn't dream of discouraging his socialist revolution. He has real faith in it, and it absorbs his vital force—he must go through with it. He talks so well about it that he *almost* makes me believe in it. I

[1] Lowes Dickinson.

am afraid he is not happy here, and will heave a great sigh of relief when he gets away. He can't stand the lack of vitality and force in the dons. I hope he won't visit it on me in his thoughts.

(1915)   *Tuesday*

. . . Yes, the day Lawrence was with me was horrid. I got filled with despair, and just counting the moments till it was ended. Partly that was due to liver, but not wholly. Lawrence is very like Shelley—just as fine, but with a similar impatience of fact. The revolution he hopes for is just like Shelley's prophecy of banded anarchs fleeing while the people celebrate a feast of love. His psychology of people is amazingly good up to a point, but at a certain point he gets misled by love of violent colouring.

Friday evg. I dined with my Harvard pupil, (T. S.) Eliot, and his bride. I expected her to be terrible, from his mysteriousness; but she was not so bad. She is light, a little vulgar, adventurous, full of life—an artist I think he said, but I should have thought her an actress. He is exquisite and listless; she says she married him to stimulate him, but finds she can't do it. Obviously he married in order to be stimulated. I think she will soon be tired of him. She refuses to go to America to see his people, for fear of submarines. He is ashamed of his marriage, and very grateful if one is kind to her. He is the Miss Sands type of American.

(1915)

. . . Lawrence took up my time from morning till 10.30, so I couldn't write yesterday. We had a terrific argument but not a disastrous one. He attacks me for various things that I don't feel to blame about—chiefly, in effect, for having a scientific temper and a respect for fact. I will send you his written comments on my syllabus. I shall be glad to know what you think of them. He took me to see a Russian Jew, Koteliansky, and Murry and Mrs. Murry[1] —they were all sitting together in a bare office high up next door to the Holborn Restaurant, with the windows shut, smoking Russian cigarettes without a moment's intermission, idle and cynical. I thought Murry *beastly* and the whole atmosphere of the three dead and putrefying.

Then we went to the Zoo—the baboon gave me much cynical

[1] John Middleton Murry and Katherine Mansfield.

satisfaction: he looked long and deliberately at everybody, and then slowly showed his teeth and snarled, with inconceivable hatred and disgust. Swift would have loved him. Then we went up to Hampstead, to the Radfords, where Mrs. Lawrence was staying. I was dead tired after the first hour, as we began arguing at once. I told Lawrence that I thought we ought to be independent of each other, at any rate at first, and not try to start a school. When he talks politics he seems to me so wild that I could not formally work with him. I hope he won't be hurt. He did not seem to be, as I put it very carefully. He is undisciplined in thought, and mistakes his wishes for facts. He is also muddle-headed. He says 'facts' are quite unimportant, only 'truths' matter. London is a 'fact' not a 'truth'. But he wants London pulled down. I tried to make him see that that would be absurd if London were unimportant, but he kept reiterating that London doesn't really exist, and that he could easily make people see it doesn't, and then they would pull it down. He was so confident of his powers of persuasion that I challenged him to come to Trafalgar Square at once and begin preaching. That brought him to earth and he began to shuffle. His attitude is a little mad and not quite honest, or at least very muddled. He has not learnt the lesson of individual impotence. And he regards all my attempts to make him acknowledge facts as mere timidity, lack of courage to think boldly, self-indulgence in pessimism. When one gets a glimmer of the facts into his head, as I did at last, he gets discouraged, and says he will go to the South Sea Islands, and bask in the sun with six native wives. He is tough work. The trouble with him is a tendency to mad exaggeration.

(1915)   *Thursday evg.*

. . . Lawrence, as was to be foreseen, is disgusted with my lecture-syllabus—it is not mystical and Blakeish enough for him. He says one ought to live from the 'impulse towards the truth' which he says is fundamentally in all of us. It seems to me, in him, merely an impulse to mistake his imagination for the truth. He talks of a desire for one-ness with others which he believes to be the same as the 'impulse to truth'. I don't believe these things exist in most people. But I find those who have a strong imagination generally read their own natures into other people, instead of getting at other people by impartial observation. Lawrence is just as ferocious a critic as Wittgenstein, but I thought W. right and I think L. wrong. He is coming to see me Sat. and I dread it. I don't know whether I shall still be able to feel any faith in my own ideas after arguing with him, although my reason is all against him. He is lacking in humour; he takes my irony seriously, and protests against it.

. . . What is wrong with mere opposition to war is that it is negative. One must find other outlets for people's wildness, and not try to produce people who have no wildness. It is all very puzzling.

I am depressed, partly by Lawrence's criticism. I feel a worm, a useless creature, sometimes I enumerate my capacities, and wonder why I am not more use in the world. I suppose scepticism is my real trouble. It is always only by an act of will that I keep it under and it weakens me.

Postmark 19th July '15.   *Monday mg. In the train.*

The visit to the Lawrences is safely over. I am glad I went, it was really not trying. I mind her much more when you are about. Lawrence wrote you a long letter yesterday, but she possessed herself of it and tore it up. Then he wrote another, which I hope will reach you. He was *very* angry. She appeared on the little wall by the flower-bed, jeering. He said, 'Come off that, lass, or I'll hit thee in the mouth. You've gone too far this time.'

He has a very profound and wise admiration for you. He keeps saying you are a priestess, a Cassandra, and that your tragedy is to have never found the god Apollo. He is quite right. He *feels* all your quality as no one else seems to. It makes me love him. I don't think, tho', that he knows that kindness is as deep as anything in you.

We talked of a plan of lecturing in the autumn on his religion, politics in the light of religion, and so on. I believe something might be made of it. I could make a splendid course on political ideas: morality, the State, property, marriages, war, taking them to their roots in human nature, and showing how each is a prison for the infinite in us. And leading on to the hope of a happier world. . . . Lawrence is *splendid*. I like his philosophy *very much* now that I have read more. It is only the beginning that is poor.

To Garsington
Postmark London, 29 Oct. '15   *Thursday night.*

I *was* glad to get your letter, I had begun to feel anxious. I am glad Lawrence was so wonderful. I have no doubt he is right to go, but I couldn't desert England. I simply *cannot bear* to think that England is entering on its autumn of life—it is too much anguish. I will not believe it, and I will believe there is health and vigour in the nation somewhere. It is all hell now, and shame—but I believe the very shame will in the end wake a new spirit. The more England goes down and down, the more profoundly I want to help, and the more I feel tied to England for good or ill. I cannot write of other things, they seem so small in comparison.

Your
B.

Greatham, Pulborough, Sussex.
Wednesday.[1]

Thank you very much for the books and your letter. You shouldn't say you are afraid of writing dull things. They are not dull. The feeling that comes out of your letter is like the scent of flowers, so generous and reassuring. It is no good now, thinking that to understand a man from his own point of view is to be happy about him. I can imagine the mind of a rat, as it slithers along in the dark, pointing its sharp nose. But I can never feel happy about it, I must always want to kill it. It contains a principle of evil. There *is* a principle of evil. Let us acknowledge it once and for all. I saw it so plainly in K. at Cambridge, it made me sick. I am sick with the knowledge of the prevalence of evil, as if it were some insidious disease.

I have been reading Dostoevsky's *Idiot*. I don't like Dostoevsky. He is again like the rat, slithering along in hate, in the shadows, and, in order to belong to the light, professing love, all love. But his nose is sharp with hate, his running is shadowy and rat-like, he is a will fixed and gripped like a trap. He is not nice.

The Cannans are here. I must say I rather love them. Strangely enough I feel a real, unalterable power for good in Gilbert. But he is very crude, very shockingly undisciplined, and consequently

---

[1] The following letters from D. H. Lawrence were written during the strange and unstable intimacy between the two men.

inarticulate. He is not *very* passionate. But he is a power for good, nevertheless, and I like him to be with us. Mary is rather nice too; she *is* rather a dear, but shallow. I like Gilbert, I am glad of his existence.

Bertie Russell will come next Thursday, to stay till Saturday. Will you let us know when you will come? You choose your own day.

Love from Frieda and me,
D. H. LAWRENCE.

Greatham, Pulborough, Sussex.
Thursday.

We shall be most glad to have a place we can always come to. And if you have need of the cottage, you will tell us at once. I know I shall be restless all my life. If I had a house and home I should become wicked. I hate any thought of possessions sticking on to me like barnacles, at once I feel destructive. And wherever I am, after a while I begin to ail me to go away.

I believe you, that love is all. But it is not easy. If I love a man, and a dog bites him, I must hate the dog. But if I must love the dog? And if I love my fellow-men, how must I feel, say, about Cambridge? Must I take hope and faith? But if I have toothache I don't depend on hope or faith or love, but on surgery. And surgery is pure hate of the defect in the loved thing. And it is surgery we want, Cambridge wants, England wants, I want. There is in us what the common people call 'proud flesh'—i.e., mortified flesh; which must be cut out; it cannot be kissed out, nor hoped out, nor removed by faith. It must be removed by surgery. And it is in us now 'proud flesh'.

I thought the War would surgeon us. Still it may. But this England at home is as yet entirely unaffected, entirely unaware of the mortification in its own body. It takes a dodge to protect its own fester from being touched; preserve your ill from touch or knowledge; that is the motto.

'If thine eye offend thee, pluck it out.' It has all been said before, plainly. It is all there, for every man to hear. But if no man wants to hear? Will cajolery or the toleration of love affect him? Curse him, let him die, and let us look to the young. That is all the faith and hope one can have—or even love.

Our love to you,
D. H. LAWRENCE.

61

D. H. Lawrence Speaks

Greatham, Pulborough, Sussex.
Sunday.

I send you what is done of my philosophy. Tell me what you think, exactly.

Bertie Russell is here. I feel rather glad at the bottom, because we are rallying to a point. I do want him to work in the knowledge of the Absolute, in the knowledge of Eternity. He *will*—apart from philosophical mathematics—be so temporal, so immediate. He won't let go, he won't act in the eternal things, when it comes to men and life. He is coming to have a real, actual, logical belief in Eternity, and upon this he can work: a belief in the absolute, an existence in the Infinite. It is very good and I am very glad.

We think to have a lecture hall in London in the autumn, and give lectures: he on Ethics, I on Immortality. Also to have meetings, to establish a little society or body around a *religious belief, which leads to action.* We must centre in the knowledge of the Infinite, of God. Then from this centre each one of us must work to put the temporal things of our own natures and of our own circumstances in accord with the Eternal God we know. You must be president. You must preside over our meetings. You must be the centre-pin that holds us together, and the needle which keeps our direction constant, always towards the Eternal things. We *mustn't* lapse into temporality.

Murry must come in, and Gilbert—and perhaps Campbell.[1] We can all lecture, at odd times. Murry has a genuine side to his nature, so has Mrs. Murry. Don't mistrust them. They are valuable, I know.

We must have some meetings at Garsington. Garsington must be the retreat where we come together and knit ourselves together. Garsington is wonderful for that. It is like the Boccaccio place where they told all the *Decameron.* That wonderful lawn, under the ilex trees, with the old house and its exquisite old front—it is *so* remote, so perfectly a small world to itself, where one *can* get away from the temporal things to consider the big things. We must draw together. Russell and I have really got somewhere. We must bring the Murrys in. Don't be doubtful of them. And

[1] Gordon Campbell, husband of Beatrice Campbell. He became Lord Glenavy. She was a painter, and published a book called *Today We Only Gossip.*

62

Frieda will come round soon. It is the same thing with her as with all the Germans—all the world—she hates the Infinite, my immortality. But she will come round.

I *know* what great work there is for us all to do in the autumn and onwards. Mind you keep your strength for it and we must really put aside the smaller personal things, and really live together in the big impersonal world as well: that must be our real place of assembly, the immortal world, the heaven of the great angels.

Send my philosophy on to Gilbert, will you? And tell me if you like it.

Don't be sad. We are only sad for a little while. At the bottom one *knows* the eternal things and is glad.

My love to Julian and to you. My warm regards to Morrell—remember me to Maria, and to Miss Sands, and Miss Hudson.[1] I trust in you entirely in this eternal belief.

D. H. Lawrence.

Greatham, Pulborough.
Monday.

I was in London this week-end for two days. Bertie Russell told me about your eyes. I was *very* sorry. You must keep very still, and not think about troublesome things. I wish I could have come to Garsington. But I can't neglect my teachings, for the short time longer it lasts.

I rather quarrelled with Russell's lectures. He won't accept in his philosophy the Infinite, the Boundless, the Eternal, as the real starting point and I think, whosoever will really set out on the journey towards Truth and the real end must do this, now. But I didn't quarrel with him. We have almost sworn *blutbrüderschaft*. We will set out together, he and I. We shall really be doing something, in the autumn. I want you to believe always.

As for my philosophy, I shall write it again, and we will talk about it when I see you.

I really think I shall give some lectures on Eternity. I shrink from it very much. I am very shy, publicly. I hate publicity of all sorts. I am safe and remote, when I write. It will be horrible to stand up and say the things I feel most vitally before an

[1] Ethel Sands and Nan Hudson, two rich American ladies who were accomplished painters. The former appears prominently in parts of the first volume.

audience. But I think it must be done. I think I shall do it. I don't know. There is a little fog between me and the autumn. I must wait for the impulse really to be born. But I think I shall be speaking. God help me, I would rather have done anything else. I would like to be remote, in Italy, writing my soul's words. To have to speak in the body is a violation to me—you don't know how much. However, anything for the new infinite relation that must come to pass.

Vale,

D. H. LAWRENCE.

Greatham, Pulborough, Sussex.
9 July 1915.

I wonder if you got the boxes I sent off the other day, and if you liked them. I wonder if this queer unsettled weather affects your health. I hope you are well.

I am just going to London for the week-end to see about furnishing the flat. Frieda has been up for several days. We should come back on Sunday evening. I shall see Russell and we shall talk about the scheme of lectures. He sent me a synopsis of a set of lectures on Political Ideas. But as yet he stands too much on the shore of this existing world. He must get into a boat and preach from out of the waters of eternity, if he is going to do any good. But I hope he isn't angry with me.

There are three weeks more here—three weeks today I have finished. Then I go to London, and we come to Garsington. I feel, when we leave here, there is the entry upon a new epoch. I am quite afraid, I feel as if I would run away—I don't know from what. But one can't run away from fate. The thought of fate makes me grin in my soul with pleasure: I am so glad it is inevitable, even if it bites off my nose.

I have broken down in the middle of my philosophy—I suppose I shall go on later when I am freer. I am correcting the proofs of *The Rainbow*. Whatever else it is, it is the voyage of discovery towards the real and eternal and unknown land. We are like Columbus, we have our backs upon Europe, till we come to the new world.

I must go now to teach the child—in three weeks we leave here, it is finished.

Au revoir,

D. H. LAWRENCE.

Could anything have made these two fine passionate men work together for the country and the causes they both so desired? I doubt it—they were both too self-centred and too intolerant of criticism. But when Bertie was writing *Social Reconstruction* they were often together, and Bertie has since told me that he was certainly stimulated by Lawrence's ideas and introduced some of them into his book. But when Bertie showed the manuscript to Lawrence, his denunciation of it was so violent that Bertie nearly destroyed it, as Lawrence urged him to do. No, their friendship was not a lasting one. There was an instinctive enmity between the natural, impatient, and not profoundly educated man of genius, and the man who was also a genius in another sphere, where mind was the produce of long inherited leisure and discipline—an aristocrat, in fact, who possessed a mind that was a fine and delicate instrument, trained and disciplined in a university where it had had stimulating contacts with other learned men. It was true that Bertie was as great a rebel as Lawrence was, but his rebellion was a more rational one, not the wild, prophetic fury of Lawrence. And though both of them were fond of dominating, and both were convinced that they were infallibly right, Bertie was not in the habit of submitting himself intellectually to anyone.

Lawrence was very poor, month after month as the War went on he became more and more baffled, discouraged, tortured and jangled in nerves. His imagination made him realize the sufferings of it to the full. His prophetic instincts urged him on to denounce this great disaster, but he found—as others found—that he was powerless to turn aside the avalanche that was sweeping all good life before it. It was difficult for anyone like him and Bertie who, as I have said, were both 'dominators' to realize their own apparent futility and powerlessness. Raw and jangled nerves led to criticism, and Lawrence wrote Bertie a violent and cruel letter, which, in the state of mind was a cruel blow. After reading it Bertie sat still, quite stunned, for a whole day—he was deeply horrified, for his belief in Lawrence's insight was still unshaken, and he thought it must be true.

This letter really separated them for ever.

Perhaps there was some grain of truth in what he said—and for that reason it hurt profoundly—but it was not an appropriate time for such an attack. Perhaps the desire for domination that existed in both of these passionate and tragic men arose

from an unsatisfied paternal instinct. In Bertie it found its outlet
later in children of his own and in a school, but in Lawrence it
continued to be unsatisfied, and laid its hand in would-be bless-
ing on many a willing or unwilling head. But without it would
he have been the novelist he was? Were not the novels filled with
his pliant children, whom he manipulated and who obeyed
their creator and did not resent his drastic treatment. He, who
orders this imaginary vivid obedient world is perhaps unfitted
to manipulate living self-willed human beings. Lawrence felt
other people's lives with such intensity that the feeling was
almost an obsession. I find in my Journal at a somewhat later
date this passage:

'Lawrence identifies himself as completely with people he
meets and for a time seems to enter into their skins and sympathe-
tically lives their lives. This is upsetting to them for he can seldom
leave them as they are, his interest penetrates and envelopes
them encouraging, stimulating, inspiring, but after a time he
begins to strip them bare of their reserve and he penetrates into
their secret life and then starts to recreate them into beings after
his own heart. This often entails violence of speech. In his own
home, I suppose, he was accustomed to give and return violent
attacks and to brush them aside in an hour and he does not
realize that other people are unable to do this. His creative
instinct never slumbers, he is never content with writing novels
or dealing with an imaginary world. He deliberately wants to
influence "real life"—and he is always being impelled to dash
out into the Market Place, and by preaching, teaching and
lashing, to recreate existing society. He has the schoolmaster,
preacher, "Messiah" instinct very strongly developed, and naturally he finds many of his pupils "self-willed", perverse, resentful
of his interference or even inert and self-satisfied, longing to be
left alone.

'With his impatience and quick resentments he, of course,
doesn't know all about them, and he then has a violent reaction.
Disappointed and resentful he suffers a psychological indigestion,
and the poor individual about whom he has been so hopeful and
enthusiastic turns sour in his spirit and is spewed out of his
mouth. He is also singularly naïve, and with all his clearness and
intensity and vision he seems to me to have a strange lack of
judgement and wisdom. One sees this in the absurdly unlikely
people he asked to come with him and join his colony in Florida.

He is, I suppose, too impetuous, intolerant and impatient for these ruminating virtues.'

> *1 Byron Villas,*
> *Vale of Health,*
> *Hampstead, London.*
> *14th Sept. 1915.*

My dear Lady Ottoline,

I send you a few leaflets about our paper. If you or Morrell could get a few people who really care, to take it, I should be very glad. But only people who care about this life now and in the future.

Today I wrote very violently to Russell. I am glad, because it had to be said sometime. But also I am very sorry, and feel like going into a corner to cry, as I used to do when I was a child. But there seems so much to cry for, one doesn't know where to begin. And then, damn it all, why should one.

> Viele Grüsse,
> D. H. LAWRENCE.

Tell those two American ladies, near you, whom I went to see, that I expect them to have my paper, because of what it says.

To Bertrand Russell:

> *1 Byron Villas,*
> *Vale of Health,*
> *Hampstead, N.W.*
> *14th Sept. 1915.*

Dear Russell,

I'm going to quarrel with you again. You simply don't speak the truth, you simply are not sincere. The article you send me is a plausible lie, and I hate it. If it says some true things, that is not the point. The fact is that you, in the essay, are all the time a lie.

Your basic desire is the maximum of desire of war, you are really the super-war-spirit. What you want is to jab and strike, like the soldier with the bayonet, only you are sublimated into words. And you are like a soldier who might jab man after man with his bayonet, saying, 'This is for ultimate peace.' The soldier would be a liar. And it isn't in the least true that you, your basic self, want ultimate peace. You are satisfying it in a direct and honourable way, saying, 'I hate you all, liars and swine, and am out to set upon you,' or stick to mathematics, where you can be true. But to come as the angel of peace—no, I prefer Tirpits a thousand times in that role.

You are simply full of repressed desires, which have become savage and anti-social. And they come out in this sheep's clothing of peace propaganda. As a woman said to me, who had been to one of your meetings: 'It seemed to me so strange with his face looking so evil, to be talking about peace and love. He can't have *meant* what he said.'

I believe in your inherent power for realizing the truth. But I don't believe in your will, not for a second. Your will is false and cruel. You are too full of devilish repressions to be anything but lustful and cruel. I would rather have the German soldiers with rapine and cruelty, than you with your words of goodness. It is the falsity I can't bear. I wouldn't care if you were six times a murderer, so long as you said to yourself, 'I am this.' The enemy of all mankind, you are, full of the lust of enmity. It is *not* the hatred of falsehood which inspires you. It is the hatred of people, of flesh and blood. It is a perverted mental blood-lust. Why don't you own it.

Let us become strangers again, I think it is better.

D. H. LAWRENCE.

CHAPTER VII

More Letters from Lawrence. Aldous Huxley Appears

In November of this year 1915, Lawrence came again to Garsington, indeed he came several times before the end of the year, sometimes alone, sometimes with Frieda. The visits when he was alone were far the happiest for him and for us all, as he was then quiet and natural. He helped me plant yew hedges, and purple irises too, about which he wrote the letter printed on p. 73.

He loved the touch and the smell of the dark clay, and the manual labour was natural and calming to his over-troubled soul. On an earlier visit he had made up his mind that a little arbour would be nice in one corner of the garden. Wood, nails appeared in a moment and in a few hours it was firmly erected. Climbing roses were planted to cover it, and Lawrence gave orders to the roses to flower with all their essential and primitive Rose-Force as rapidly and abundantly as possible, and to raise themselves up from the dark earth into sunshine. The little arbour was always preserved and propped up for the sake of the man who planned and built it, much to the annoyance of others who thought it absurd and suburban.

In the evenings he would read to us poems, generally poems from Swinburne, or he would tell some story from his own life, making the characters often so comic, and kindly and real, that one felt one was taking part in the scenes he described. We also went into Oxford and looked at the colleges, and museums; he felt it all 'dead and useless', but he enjoyed very much looking at the old illumined missals and books in the Bodleian, and we pored over them enjoying the fun and their grotesqueness. I got the librarian to take them out of the cases for him to see, as he wanted to copy some. It was enchanting being with anyone so sympathetic—he had that wonderful child quality of excitement over small things as well as over great ones. I had seldom met anyone that I felt so lovable.

One wet day, we (Mademoiselle Juliette Baillot and Maria Nys, Julian and the Gilbert Cannans) were all whirled into acting a play—Lawrence's magnetism made us all forget ourselves and we became the characters that Lawrence apportioned to us. He himself was Othello, in a large straw hat and a real Arab coat. It was the only time I ever saw him look beautiful. I well remember, even at the time, realizing how happy, fresh and gay I felt. We had all been liberated from our self-consciousness, and had had one afternoon's perfect freedom and gaiety.

Another day he was absorbed in copying most beautifully a Persian miniature, which I think he gave to Mrs. Cannan. Lawrence's vitality and presence seemed to make every moment of the day throb with its own intense life, so that whatever one did with him was right and perfect to do. At this moment the memory I have of these days makes me see how rare that feeling is—how seldom one can look back and relive scenes without some regret.

But such happy good times do not last. The horror of war grew worse and worse and reverberated in Lawrence and nearly drove him mad. I had many letters from him about now, but the following are about his visits to Garsington; also a short description of Garsington that he wrote about now and sent to me in a letter:

Garsington. *1 December 1915.*

So vivid a vision, everything so visually poignant, it is like that concentrated moment when a drowning man sees all his past crystallized into one jewel of recollection.

The slow, reluctant, pallid morning, unwillingly releasing its tarnished embellishment of gold, far off there, outside, beyond the shafted windows, beyond, over the forgotten unseen country, that lies sunken in gloom below, whilst the dawn sluggishly bestirs itself, far off, beyond the window-shafts of stone, dark pillars, like bars, dark and unfathomed, set near me, before the reluctance of the far-off dawn.

The window-shafts, like pillars, like bars, the shallow Tudor arch looping over between them, looping the darkness in a pure edge, in front of the far-off reluctance of the dawn.

Shafted, looped windows between the without and the within, the old house, the perfect old intervention of fitted stone, fitted

70

perfectly about a silent soul, the soul that in drowning under this last wave of time looks out clear through the shafted windows to see the dawn of all dawns taking place, the England of all recollection rousing into being.

The wet lawn drizzled with brown, sodden leaves, the feathery heap of the ilex tree; the garden-seat all wet and reminiscent.

Between the ilex tree and the bare, purplish elms, a gleaming segment of all England, the dark plough-land and wan grass, and the blue, hazy heap of the distance, under the accomplished morning.

So the day has taken place, all the visionary business of the day. The young cattle stand in the straw of the stack yard, the sun gleams on their white fleece, the eyes of Io, and the man with side-whiskers carries more yellow straw into the compound. The sun comes in all down one side, and above, in the sky, all the gables and the grey stone chimney-stacks are floating in pure dreams.

There is threshed wheat smouldering in the great barn, the fire of life; and the sound of the threshing machine, running, drumming.

The threshing machine, running, drumming, waving its steam in a corner of a great field, the rapid nucleus of darkness beside the yellow ricks: and the rich plough-land comes up, ripples up in endless grape-coloured ripples, like a tide of procreant desire; the machine sighs and drums, wind blows the chaff in little eddies, blows the clothes of the men on the ricks close against their heaven, their limbs blown clean in contour, naked shapely animated fragments of earth active in heaven.

Coming home, by the purple and crimson hedges, red with berries, up hill over the heavy ground to the stone, old three-pointed house with its raised chimney-stacks, the old manor lifting its fair pure stone amid trees and foliage, rising from the lawn, we pass the pond where white ducks hastily launch upon the lustrous dark grey waters.

So to the steps up the porch, through the doorway, and into the interior, fragrant with all the memories of old age, and of by-gone, remembered lustiness.

It is the vision of a drowning man, the vision of all that I am, all I have become, and ceased to be. It is me, generations and generations me, every complex, gleaming fibre of me, every lucid pang of my coming into being. And oh, my God, I cannot bear it. For it is not this me who am drowning swiftly under this last wave of time, this bursten flood.

But in the farmyard up the hill, I remember, there were clusters of turkeys that ruffled themselves like flowers suddenly ruffled into blossom, and made strange, unacquainted noises, a foreign tongue, exiles of another life.

In Florida they will go in droves in the shadow, like metallic clouds, like flowers with red pistils drooping in the shade, under the quivering, quick, miraculous roof of pine-needles, or drifting between the glowing pine trunks, metallic birds, or perched at evening like cones on the red-hot pine boughs, or bursting in the morning across open glades of sunshine, like flowers burst and taking wing.

There is a morning which dawns like an iridescence on the wings of sleeping darkness, till the darkness bursts and flies off in glory, dripping with the rose of morning.

There is the soaring suspense of day, dizzy with sunshine, and night flown away and utterly forgotten.

There is evening coming to settle amid the red-hot bars of the pine trunks, dark cones, that emit the utter, electric darkness.

Another dawn, another day, another night—another heaven and earth—a resurrection.

D. H. LAWRENCE.

1 Byron Villas,
Vale of Health,
Hampstead, London.
Friday.

We should like to come to Garsington on Monday, and stay till Thursday. On Friday Frieda must go to the dentist.

I haven't asked the Murrys, because I think I would rather we came alone. But if you have asked them, separately, to come with us, very good.

Today I have got our passports. I feel as if really we were going to America—and *soon.* We may go to Florida for this winter. I must see if I can get some money, that is all. But I can, I think, all right . . .

I feel awfully queer and trembling in my spirit, because I am going away from the land and the nation I have belonged to: departing, emigrating, changing the land of my soul as well as my mere domicile. It is rather terrible, a form of death. But I feel as if it were my fate.

I must: to live!

Yours

D. H. LAWRENCE.

(Written after a visit to Garsington when he had come alone—without Frieda.)

1 Byron Villas,
Vale of Health,
Hampstead, London.
Thursday.

I arrived home safely, in the rain, with my Hessians and my flowers. London *does* strike a blow at the heart, I must say: tonight, in a black rain out of doors, and a Tube full of spectral, decayed people. How much better and more beautiful the country is—you are very wise to be at Garsington.

Frieda is delighted with the flowers, and my wonderful boots, and with the thought of the embroidery. What queer things to come home with! I hope the Hessians are seven-leagued boots that will carry me to the ends of the earth; to the Blessed Isles to the undiscovered lands whose fruits are all unknown to us.

I am very glad I came down. It will always be a sort of last vision of England to me—the beauty of England, the wonder of this terrible autumn, when we set the irises above the pond in the stillness and wetness.

How cruel it is that the world should so have come to an end, this world, our world, whilst we still live in it, that we must either die or go away dispossessed, exiled in body and spirit.

Remember me to Julian and Philip. I hope all the flowers will grow and be beautiful. We shall see you again soon.

D. H. LAWRENCE.

1 Byron Villas,
Vale of Health,
Hampstead, N.W.
1 Sept. 1915.

One can't help the silences that intervene nowadays, it must be so. But I think they are times when new things are born, and like winter, when trees are rid of their old leaves, to start again. It is the New Year one wants so badly; let the old die together, completely. It is only the new spring I care about, opening the hard little buds that seems like stone, in the souls of the people. They must open and a new world begin. But first there is the shedding of the old, which is so slow and so difficult, like a sickness. I find it is so difficult to let the old life go, and to wait for the new life to take form. But it begins to take form now. It is not any more such a fierce question of shedding away.

I always want us to be friends, real friends in the deep, honourable, permanent sense. But it is very difficult for me to be clear and true to my deepest self. We must allow first of all for the extreme lapses in ourselves. But the little hard buds of a new world are not destroyed. I do believe in our permanent friendship, something not temporal.

Russell and I have parted for a little while, but it is only in the natural course. The real development continues even in its negation, under the winter.

Postmark 15 Nov. '15.

1 Byron Villas,
Vale of Health,
Hampstead, London.
Monday.

I am posting to you a pack of MS, including that of *The Rainbow*. If you don't want it you can have it burnt, otherwise it might lie at Garsington till it is worth the selling. I don't want to see it any more.

We are getting ready to go. I have made all enquiries, preparatory to booking, to sail on the 24th of this month. We shall have to hurry to get things done. We shall go next Tuesday to see my people in Derbyshire, and on from there to Liverpool the next day. I feel very strange and abstracted, preparing to go.

I am writing to Russell to ask him if he will come and see us this week.

I shall always look to you as being a sort of spiritual home in England for me, for us. It makes it very much easier to go, that you are there, to be in connection with us, wherever we are. You on this shore, we on that, and the true connection between us.

You will come to see us. Frieda sends her love, with mine.

D. H. LAWRENCE.

I rather liked Clive Bell—not deeply. He says it is tragic that you can never have any *real* connection with anybody. I did not say that there *was* a real connection between you and me. Let them not know. But there *is* a bond between us, in spirit, deep to the bottom.

D.H.L.

1 Byron Villas,
Vale of Health,
Hampstead, N.W.
12 Dec. 1915.

Thank you for the letter and the pound. The last I *did not want*.

I hear Heseltine and Kouzoumdjian are coming to you to-morrow. Heseltine is a bit backboneless and needs stiffening up. But I like him very much; Kouzoumdjian seems a bit blatant and pushing, you may be put off him. But that is because he is *very foreign*, even though he doesn't know it himself. In English life he is in a strange, alien medium, and he can't adjust himself. But I find the love of him *very good*. One must be patient with his jarring manner, and listen to the sound decency that is in him. He is not a bit rotten, which most young cultivated Englishmen are.

Murry is back, and I am rather out of sympathy with him. Bertie came. He is growing *much better*; he is going to become young and new. I have more hopes.

Don't trust Brett very much; I think she doesn't quite tell the truth about herself to you. She is very satisfied as she is, really very satisfied. She is one of the 'sisters' of this life, her role is always to be a sister.

We leave here on the 20th, go to my sister's in Derbyshire for Christmas, and then I don't know where, I must say I feel again a certain amount of slow, subterranean hope. It won't put forth any leaves, nor show any activity yet, I believe: but it seems to be full and nascent somewhere in the underneath of my soul. Probably we shall go to the West—Devon, Somerset— for a while after Christmas, I don't know. I must let things work themselves into being. One can do nothing now, forcing is disastrous. I shall not go to America until a stronger force from there pulls me across the sea. It is not a case of my will.

I went to a recruiting station yesterday to be attested and to get a military exemption. But I hated it so much, after waiting nearly two hours, that I came away. And yet, waiting there in the queue, I felt the *men* were very decent, and that the slumbering lion was going to wake up in them: not against the Germans either, but against the great lie of this life. I felt all the men were decent, even the police and the officials. It was at Battersea Town Hall. A strange, patient spirit possessed everybody, as under a doom, a bad fate superimposed. But I felt the patience rested upon slumbering strength, not exhaustion, and the strength would begin before long to stretch itself like a waking lion. I felt, though I *hated* the situation almost to *madness*, so vile and false and degrading, such an utter travesty of action on my part, waiting even to be attested that I might be rejected, still I felt, when suddenly I broke out of the queue, in face of the table where one's name was to be written, and went out across the hall away from all the underworld of this spectral submission and climbed on a bus, and after a while saw the fugitive sunshine across the river on the spectral sunlit towers at Westminster, that I had triumphed, like Satan flying over the world and knowing he had won at last, though he had not come into even a fragment of his own. I feel somewhere that the triumph is mine, remote, oh very remote, and buried underground, but the triumph is mine. It is only the immediate present which frightens me and bullies me. In the long run I have the victory; for all those men in the queue, for those spectral, hazy, sunny towers hovering beyond the river, for the world that is to be. Endless patient strength and courage, that is all that is necessary—and the avoiding of disaster.

Let me only be still, and know we can force nothing, and compel nothing, can only nourish in the darkness the unuttered buds of the new life that shall be. That is our life now: this nourishing of the germs, the unknown quicks when the new life is coming into being in us and in others, I have hope of Bertie too—only patience, only patience, and endless courage to reject false dead things and false killing processes.

With love from Frieda and me,
                                    D. H. LAWRENCE.

On December 3rd, 1915, I find the following entry:

'Lawrence and Frieda have been here again, and they brought with them Philip Heseltine, a musician, and Kouzoumdjian ("Michael Arlen"), also an Indian called Sarawadi, who is at Oxford, and who is a friend of Heseltine. What strange creatures Lawrence and Frieda attract to themselves. He is enthusiastic about both Heseltine and Kouzoumdjian, but I don't feel attracted to them, indeed quite the reverse. Heseltine is tall and blonde, soft and so degenerate that he seems somehow corrupt. Kouzoumdjian is a fat dark-blooded tight-skinned Armenian Jew, and though Lawrence believes that he will be a great writer, I find it hard to believe. Obviously he has a certain vulgar sexual force, but he is very coarse-grained and conceited. I cannot sit in the room with them for long. He and Heseltine seem to pollute the atmosphere, and stifle me, and I have to escape from their presence—also I get very tired of the continual boasting of what they are going to do. They flatter Frieda and pay her more attention than they do Lawrence, so naturally they are both great geniuses in her eyes, and she is enthusiastic about them— they are going down to Cornwall when the Lawrences go there. I do not understand the Indian Sarawadi. He is extremely anti-English, but like all Indians quite foreign and remote, though he seems more substantial and self-confident than most of his race.

'Frieda is devilish, and she really is a wild beast, quite uncontrolled, cruel to Lawrence, and madly jealous if she thinks anyone esteems Lawrence more than her.'

When I wrote this about Kouzoumdjian I little thought that he would develop into the successful novelist 'Michael Arlen'. I have never met him again since this time, but I constantly wear a little yellow shawl that he sent me, as he remarked that I was fond of yellow. And much as I felt repelled by him at that time I expect he is a kind man. I have always heard that when Lawrence was ill and poor he pressed financial help upon him—which Lawrence refused.

These visits to Garsington seemed like a lull before the most stormy time in Lawrence's life. Frieda had begun to growl and paw the ground. She was very much annoyed that he and I had so much in common—politics, love of England, poetry—and she became violently jealous of what she thought was my influence over him. In a letter to me she said:

77

'I would not mind if you and he had an ordinary love-affair—what I hate is this "soul-mush".'[1]

She became more and more infuriated that I was detached from her, and she saw that she didn't impress me. I find an entry in my Journal:

'Frieda is turning Lawrence against Bertie Russell, because Bertie doesn't admire and flatter her, so she has made Lawrence mistrust him. She is certainly a sister to Potiphar's wife. She is turning him against me, for she tells him that I have been rude and contemptuous of her, and did not treat her with enough respect when she was here. So now he is angry with me, and writes to me about it. I am very unhappy about it, but she is so outrageous that I cannot bring myself to eat humble pie to her. I wrote her a nice letter but she even complains of that, and answered that my letter was impudent and an insult.'

It was, I believe, about this time that my mother-in-law told me that a young man at Balliol wanted very much to come and see us, and wanted me to invite him out. She said he was related to some of her old Oxford friends, and that he had the charming name of Aldous. I accordingly wrote a polite little note to the young man, Aldous Huxley, to ask him out to luncheon on Sunday.

A very thin, very tall, delicate young man, with a very beautiful serious face arrived, dressed in a corduroy coat and cut breeches and stockings. His eyesight was very bad, which made him stoop in order to view things closely. He was rather silent and aloof, and I felt as he sat on during the afternoon that he was rather bored, for we happened to be alone that Sunday. But, whether bored or not, he soon became a frequent visitor, and converted himself into being a son of the house. For years one of the bedrooms at Garsington was known as Mr. Huxley's room. He came and met Lawrence when he was with us, and I suggested that he should go and see him at Hampstead when he was there. I think he was puzzled and rather overcome, and perhaps scared, at Lawrence's quick and immediate approach, brushing away all preliminaries—vetting him in fact, putting him under his X-ray.

[1] After Lawrence died, Frieda came to England. The Morrells, with characteristic kindness, attempted to protect her from the vultures which were gathering over the remains. Once when I met her with them, and they were talking of old days, Frieda said suddenly, in the strong German accent she was never to lose, 'Oh, I was so jealous of you, Ottoline! *Oh,* how jealous I was!' 'But Frieda,' droned Ottoline sweetly, 'there was *no* need.' 'I know!' retorted Frieda. '*That* is why I was so jealous!'

I was amused to hear that Lawrence claimed him immediately as a disciple and asked him to join 'the Colony' that he was planning in Florida. I felt how miserable Aldous, with his fastidious reserve, his delicate and perhaps over-intellectual temperament, would be if he went. Lawrence wrote:

1 Byron Villas,
Vale of Health,
Hampstead, N.W.
7 Dec. 1915.

I have written to Huxley to ask him to come here as soon as he is in London, I will see also if Brett will come to tea with us, without Gertler's omnipresent guardianship.

I also think, that perhaps, in a little while, I can unite with the very young people, to do something. But first let them try their teeth on the world, let them taste it thoroughly as it is, so that they shall be ready to reject it. I feel my going away will only be a sort of retirement to get strength and concord in myself. I am pretty sick also, and must get robust again in spirit. Also this country must go through some stages of its disease, till I am any good for it, or it is any good for me. It is full of unripe ulcers that must come out, come to a head, then perhaps they can be lanced and healed. It must work out the impurity which is now deep-seated in its blood. There is no other help for it.

Why are you so sad about your life! Only let go all this will to have things in your own control. We must all submit to be helpless and obliterated, quite obliterated, destroyed, cast away into nothingness. There is something will rise out of it, something new, that now is not. This which we are must cease to be, that we may come to pass in another being. Do not struggle with your will, to dominate your conscious life—do not do it. Only drift, and let go—let go, entirely, and become dark, quite dark—like winter which mows away all the leaves and flowers, and lets only the dark underground roots remain. Let all the leaves and flowers and arborescent form of your life be cut off and cast away, all cut off and cast away, all the old life, so that only the deep roots remain in the darkness underground, and you have no place in the light, no place at all. Let all knots be broken, all bonds unloosed, all connections slackened and released, like the trees which release their leaves, and the plants which die away utterly

79

above ground, let go all their being and pass away, only sleep in the profound darkness where being takes place again.

Do not keep your will in your conscious self. Forget, utterly forget, and let go. Let your will lapse back into your unconscious self, so you move in a sleep, and in darkness, without sight or understanding. Only then will you act straight from the dark source of life, outwards, which is creative life. I tell this to you, I tell it to myself—to let go, to release from my will everything that my will would hold, to lapse back into darkness and unknowing. There must be deep winter before there can be spring.

I will let you know when anything happens to our plans. Only do not struggle, let go and become dark, quite dark.

D. H. LAWRENCE.

And again, after he had seen him, he wrote:
I liked Huxley very much. He will come to Florida.
This is also a letter from Aldous at the same time:

Sunday 1916.   *27 Westbourne Square, W.*

Dear Lady Ottoline,

I went to see Lawrence on Friday. One can't help being very much impressed by him. There is something almost alarming about his sincerity and seriousness—something that makes one feel oneself to be the most shameful dilettante, persifleur, waster and all the rest. Not but what I think he's wrong. All that he condemns as mere dilettantism and literary flippancy—and the force of his sincerity carries one temporarily with him—all this is something much more than an excrementitious by-product of real life. It all comes back again to the question we were talking about the other day—the enrichment of emotion by intellect. And so too with Lawrence. I'm inclined to think that he would find a life unenriched by the subtler amenities of intellect rather sterile—but I think there's a lot in his theory of the world being in a destructive, autumnal period. What seems to me questionable is, are you going to hustle on the spring by going to Florida to immure yourself with one Armenian, one German wife and, problematically, one or two other young people? It may be possible that some Pentecostal gift of inspiration may descend, and I suppose it's worth risking failure for that possibility. If,

80

as seems probable, I go and visit my Texan brother next year, I shall certainly join his colony for a bit. I think it might be very good to lead the monastic life for a little.

Meanwhile, thank you very much for B. Russell's syllabus. I should have liked to go—but see that dates are impossible. They begin just as I go back to Oxford—so I fear they are out of the question.

Yours sincerely,
ALDOUS HUXLEY.

CHAPTER VIII

New Friends: Katherine Mansfield and Middleton Murry

Disappointed and sad at the friction between Lawrence and Bertie, and the collapse of any work between them that I had so hoped for, I turned from them to thoughts of my own world, and calmed my spirit there. I find the following in my Journal in January 1916:

'How I love the black trees against the sky, vivid, poignant, bare tracery against the winter sky, and the purple hedges, red-black, as if they are already smouldering and at any moment burst into flame, into new life that is forcing itself up from the earth's centre, the fire of life.

'And how I love the brown ploughed fields all moist and wet, ready for the seed that will be scattered and crushed in.

'I have grown to love these natural things of life. They mean much more to me since I have been here, and I find purely intellectual people who are not aware of the earth and country and nature very dull. They seem almost as if they are just bodies or boxes encasing a very alert machine that is wound up each morning and tick-ticks mechanically on until it runs down in sleep. The very intense intellectuals seem only to know the pleasure of their own mental velocity—almost apart from life—and seldom do they escape from their own mechanisms or begin to be aware of beauty, of nature, or earth moods, or indeed of the richness and humour of life.

'Bertie, for instance, had very little contact with nature—he is so concentrated on the life of reason that he doesn't seem to realize the existence of all that is around him. The rigidity of his movements denotes the want of harmony and rhythm within— certainly a body is moulded by the character that grows within it. Even Lytton, when I walk with him, never seems to notice anything, and when I say, "Oh, look, isn't that beautiful?" never responds but seems annoyed.

'How exacting I am becoming. I start off by thinking this person and that person have all the qualities one needs in an intimate friend, and then when I see into them and find that at most they have but one or two ingredients I withdraw and am impatient and intolerant and blame them in my thoughts for their narrowness, their ignorance, or their want of sensibility, their unawareness. And when I hear them laying down the law about life or about things they are ignorant of—poetry or religion or art—I become even more intolerant and angry; and yet, after all, perhaps it isn't their fault. They can't help being incomplete.

'Perhaps it is a mistake to know people too well, to look into them too closely, and put them under one's own microscope, but I know I cannot dim my critical sight. I believe the real physical attraction between two people is only perfect when the riches of the character and mind have impregnated and permeated the body, and so draw another to it by an inner magnetism.

'I have been very happy here these last weeks, for I have been more or less alone, and it has enabled me to get my inner self clear and free and flowing. Solitude is essential to me and rests my nerves and helps me to branch out. I feel like a tree that is crowded and cannot grow if I have people too much upon me. I never feel dull alone, for it is so exciting when one becomes aware of one's own thoughts growing, but I suppose one needs contact with other people from time to time—the electric shock, the vibration that shakes one's own heavy winter clay. These dark sombre days of winter, and the deep-down sense of spring coming—far away, not too near, only a glimmer of the flame, not visible but just moving; this is what I feel within myself. How strong this vital new life must be that even the horrors and misery of the War cannot kill it.

'Nothing can convert me to feel that war is right. It is so obviously a violation of all civilization and of the natural growth and development of man that comes from contact and understanding between people and nations. Here is indeed a field where intelligence and reason ought to guide us. It is surely essential that individuals should be treated as sacred, until they have proved themselves pernicious. In war all reason, all right intelligence, are thrown overboard, or forced to serve brutality and destruction. And men relapse into the animal—to fight men must become brutes. No one who had not become so could go out deliberately to maim and inflict torture and death on other men, or to destroy ruthlessly beautiful buildings and land. Perhaps in old days when men fought against barbaric invasions it was less wicked, for men then were less sensitive to cruelty.'

Philip and I were hoping to make a centre at Garsington for those who were still under the control of reason, who saw the War as it really was, not through false emotional madness, and the intoxication of war fever. We hoped that they would at least meet and think and talk freely, and realize that there were other values in life.

But sometimes I used to feel hurt when people came and did not take any trouble to talk to me, but just amused themselves and ignored me. When I was talking to Gilbert Cannan one day I said that I felt that the young people who came looked on me as a sort of kind manageress of a hotel, and he rather took me aback by saying, 'Of course, we do.'

Gilbert Cannan was too self-centred and conceited to realize what other people felt—still he remained for a time a regular visitor.

One of our guests at Christmas was Lawrence's friend, J. Middleton Murry, whom Lawrence had asked me to invite, as otherwise he would have been alone in London (Katherine Mansfield with whom he was living being abroad).

I had already met him on one of my visits to the Lawrences at Greatham, but he was very silent that day and hardly spoke. He was an odd, remarkable-looking man, with rather a cavernous face, large unseeing vague dark eyes, and a slender lithe figure. He is rather like a southern Welshman. I didn't know what his history was—except that he had been at the Bluecoat School and had got a scholarship at Oxford, and was doing well there when he fell in love with Katherine Mansfield and left Oxford to go and live with her. They were not married at this time, as she was not yet divorced from her husband, Mr. Bowden. He had a romantic passion for her, and seemed quite absorbed by the thought of her. When he came to Garsington he had just left her at Bandol, but a telegram arrived from her asking him to return. He was undecided what to do, and came up to my little sitting-room to consult me. I let him talk on and on about her, telling me of their wonderful times together, their transcendental union of soul and body, and the way they 'wisped away together', as he called it—by which, I suppose, he meant flights of thought and talk. It moved me very much hearing of this lovely blending of two beings into one, and the way their minds and imagination flew through the air together. I felt that he was lost and unhappy without her, and very naturally advised him to go back to her at once (I gave him £5 for his journey). I knew he was longing for me to give him this advice, and in an hour or two I was waving him off at the gates. I felt happy thinking of his wonderful and lovely union. It was something lovely to think of in the midst of the sea of hate that surged around us like dark violent waves. I seemed in a way to share the joy . . . and feel the beauty of it in myself. It was probably as an outcome of this talk that I wrote in my diary:

'I always feel the soul within me full as if it were a living, quivering, vibrating thing like a bird—which could grow and grow and whose wings I could fold around those I love. I will protect it, and feed it and keep my bird strong. All my youth I developed it, but of late I have neglected it and only tried to develop my reason, but I don't see why they should not develop equally. I feel as if I were really a wild creature that flies with the wind and is never caught by anyone. I fly near other people but they never come to me or touch my essential self, and when they approach me I fly on. I laugh to myself and hear them say to each other, "Do you know her? Oh, yes, I know her"—but I am really far far away, free and laughing and eluding them. I like to shake myself free and press on, press on. Human friends want to keep one always the same by their side, and I want to fly on and on, rapidly, quickly. I have sung and laughed these days, so happy to be alone and free. Who is it with whom one can commune— is it only oneself? Or is it some spirit self? I know that all that is beautiful and real and of value to me exists in this spiritual world behind the visible world. Art can express it, music is its language, poetry is full of it. The practical world is always present but I am not very useful there. I know that clearness of thought and reason are essential, but they don't interfere with or destroy my other life—they cannot prove that it does or does not exist—that can only be proved by the lives of those who believe in it. I wish I could express it in words, but I cannot. The strings of one's inner life must be kept tight and in tune as the strings of a violin, and then perhaps a line of poetry or an air of Mozart or a fugue of Bach will make it vibrate and tremble with joy and ecstasy.'

As I have often mentioned Mademoiselle—or 'Mamzelle' as Brett christened her—I must say who she is.

Mademoiselle Juliette Baillot came to us to be a companion and *soi-disant* governess to Julian. The first time I saw her was at Oxford Station where we sat together on a bench—a tall, slim, very pretty, shy, severe and composed Swiss girl, with plaits of fair hair done into two buns on her ears, she seemed almost absurdly young, but she herself seemed quite confident and I wanted someone young and cheerful and active for Julian. She came and was perfect, only I afterwards found she had been rather tyrannized over by Julian. But she took part in all our life and with her lovely simplicity and intelligence wound her way in and out of the various visitors, much liked by everybody. Heseltine, D. H. Lawrence's friend, fell in love with her, but luckily she did not return it. I can never forget her lovely slim figure as she dived into the pond, her long yellow hair making her look like a water nymph or a picture of a silvery saint by Crivelli.

She remained with us until Julian went to St. Felix School, Southwold; then she returned to her aunt, Mrs. Howlett at St. James's Palace, but soon went out again to Brett's sister, the Ranee of Sarawak, to look after her daughters in Scotland. This did not last very long, for she soon became engaged to be married to Julian Huxley, Aldous's brother. He had stayed with us at Garsington when he returned from America where he had been a professor at an American university, and had met 'Mamzelle' there. Afterwards he went to Italy to work on the G.H. 2 Intelligence Dept. I think he followed her to Scotland after the War and they were married.

They lived for some time in Oxford, where he was a don at New College, then in London when he was at King's College. They are now the Head of the Zoological Gardens.

Juliette and I have always remained great friends and I know her to be one of the most loyal and faithful women that I know.

When she told Lady Mary Murray (Gilbert Murray's wife) that I was her eldest boy's Godmother, Lady Mary said, 'Isn't that very blasphemous?' A charming comment from an atheist.

CHAPTER IX

Letters from the Murrys

Soon after Christmas (1915) I received these letters from
J. Middleton Murry and Katherine Mansfield:

I am just on my way. I have only the time to say how
deeply happy I was with you at Garsington. Believe me my
gratitude is no less than yours. You have made me feel that
there is at least one place in England which is a haven for us
both; and I know that Katherine will be as happy in that knowledge as I.

> *Gare de Lyon,*
> *Paris.*
> *December 31.*

Dear Lady Ottoline,

I wrote to you in so violent a hurry that I hardly even recollect
what I said—and even if I recollected it all, I know perfectly well
that I did not express one half of what I felt on coming away
from Garsington.

One picture is vivid in my mind and will always be—of your
running to the gate and waving to me as I was driven away. I'm
sure you understand me well enough not to think it odd if I say
that your *geste* suddenly warmed my soul. Nothing like it has
happened to me for so long. I was radiant all through the journey
home, and the memory of it warms me now.

I felt at that moment that I knew you, and that I had found a
friend—well, I must use our magic word again, for *toujours*. It is
only in such a moment that I can speak for both of us with absolute certainty. We go about the world in a kind of terror. We
take no roots either in a place or in the hearts of those who call
themselves our friends. I am not whining at all—tho' Lorenzo
says I do—for it is a fair price to pay for our own secret and
transcendent happiness together. But there are times when we
suffer terribly, and times when we cannot face the suffering. So

87

we are called impossible. We make arrangements and break them. We commit every kind of social crime. It is only our method of self-defence. We dare not let our hearts be open to people who will hurt as cruelly.

And at the same time we long to be free. It may be impossible that we should share our happiness but we are hungry for the persons with whom we need conceal nothing.

We have found such a one in you. Don't think it strange that I write 'we'. You must imagine me gloriously thinking of the delight with which I will tell Katherine all about it. She will know at once all I mean and she will be as happy as I.

Yours ever,
J. M. M.

I will write to you when I get to Bandol.
For certain obvious reasons I have said that K. was very ill. Would you mind not denying it if the occasion comes?
P.S. (by Katherine Mansfield)

I have been wanting to write to you for nearly three weeks. I *have* been writing to you ever since the day when Murry came and said, 'There's a perfectly wonderful woman in England,' and told me about you. Since then I have wanted to send you things too—some anemones, purple and crimson lake and a rich, lovely white, some blue irises that I found growing in the grass, too frail to gather, certain places in the woods where I imagine you would like to be—and certain hours like this hour of bright moonlight, when the flowering almond tree hangs over our white stone verandah, a blue shadow with long tassels.

So please take, if you care for them, all these things from me as well as the letters I have not sent but have written and written to you. All that Murry tells me of you is quite wonderful and perfect, but it's strange—I feel that I *knew* it (although I denied the knowledge over and over) from the first time that I heard of you —and I felt it, even through the atmosphere of that evening at your house—when you were ever so far away. I long to meet you. Will you write to us again?

But until we do see you—will you remember that you are real and lovely to us both and that we are ever grateful to you because you are. Goodnight.'

A few days later—K.M. wrote again:

The days go by so quickly and I have wanted to write to you on nearly every separate day—and just *not* written—to say how glad we were to have a lovely letter from you and to tell you how much we both long to come and see you when we are back in England. Thank you for letting us see Frieda's letter too. I am thankful that the Armenian is gone but I wish he had taken Heseltine with him. I suspect Heseltine. I did from what Jack told me of him before I knew that he had 'confided' in Frieda. What a pity it is that dear Lorenzo sees rainbows round so many dull people and pots of gold in so many mean hearts. But he will never change.

We have decided to spend the summer with them in a farm-house somewhere near the sea—Lawrence seems to be much better—I am glad—one hates to think of him being ill.

We are leaving here at the end of April—Jack is very busy at present with the book on Dostoevsky, and I have a book on my hands too; we feel they won't be old enough to travel until then. I am awfully anxious for Jack's book to be published. It is really brilliant.

The weather has changed. All the almond flowers are gone. Our walks and climbs are over. We sit by the fire and work nearly all day. Only in the late afternoon we put on our hats and run into the wind and go down to the sea and wish that the waves would be still bigger—they're never high enough. In the evenings we read and talk and 'make plans' . . . We are awfully happy—and I know that we always shall be wherever we are together.

It made me very happy thinking of these two delightful friends who were entering into our life and who were so friendly and sympathetic.

CHAPTER X

Siegfried Sassoon

Reading *The Times* one day in January (1916) my eye caught this sonnet:

TO VICTORY
(By a Private Soldier at the Front.)

Return to greet me, colours that were my joy,
Not in the woeful crimson of men slain,
But shining as a garden: come with the streaming
Banners of dawn and sundown after rain.

I want to fill my gaze with blue and silver,
Radiance through living roses, spires of green
Rising in young-limbed copse and lovely wood
Where the hueless wind passes and cries unseen.

I am not sad; only I long for lustre,
I am tired of greys and browns and the leafless ash.
I would have hours that move like a glitter of dancers,
Far from the angry guns that boom and flash.

Return, musical, gay with blossoms and fleetness,
Days when my sight shall be clear, and my heart rejoice,
Come from the sea with breadth of approaching brightness,
When the blithe wind laughs on the hills with uplifted voice.

S.S.

   In those days when we read the papers with pain and scepticism it was almost a shock to come upon anything so sympathetic as 'I want to fill my gaze with blue and silver'. I believe the newspaper was thrown away but I retrieved it and the little yellow cutting is before me as I write. This sonnet seemed to me to have real beauty and kept 'vibrating in my memory'. I could not guess who wrote it, as S.S. was quite an unknown signature. For some days I quarrelled with myself as to whether I should write to

The Times to enquire who wrote it. At last I did so and received this letter from Edmund Gosse:

'The Editor of *The Times* has sent me your letter about the poem signed "S.S.", which I contributed. The author is a very charming, simple and enthusiastic young man, whose name is Lieut. Siegfried Sassoon, 1st Battalion Royal Welsh Fusiliers, British Expeditionary Force, France. I am sure he will very much appreciate a letter from you.

'*The Times* romanced in calling him "a Private Soldier". The fact is that he enlisted as a P.S. but has since got a 1st Lieut.'s commission. He is a nephew of Thomas Thorneycroft. He has been in the habit of sending me his verses, which have interested me a good deal, and I hope he is destined to achieve distinction.

He is extremely modest and a little *sauvage*—with a woodland wildness. He is a very fine horseman, which is an unusual merit in poets nowadays.'

So much encouraged I wrote to Siegfried Sassoon and received this note from him:

'Your letter gave me great pleasure. People don't often take the trouble to applaud a poem which they enjoy. How nice if everyone did it! The beauty and freedom have all taken flight to the wars: out here there is nothing but beauty—or perhaps one has fresh eyes to see it. I will send you a little book of my verses when I am in England on leave which will be within the next few weeks. I often stayed at Oxford, though I didn't "go" there. I love the Oxfordshire landscape, and the Gloucestershire borders, as I associate them with early summer weather and orchards in blossom.

'Do you know Mr. Gosse? He is as delightful as his studies of old (and new) poets.'

And a few days later arrived a little green paper book with his photograph inside.

I wondered if I should ever see this young poet with the hand-some face, or would he too be soon blown to atoms.

CHAPTER XI

Baroness d'Erlanger, Thomas Earp and the Lawrences

The snow in February 1916 was very deep. An odd, silent, strange world. The figures of the farm labourers and the old village men looked black and vivid as they passed our old stone gates with the tall trees behind them. They trudged home, carrying branches of firewood on their backs; and the gay companies of school children, excited and happy, with muffled up necks and stiff red hands from snowballing, gambolled past.

I was out in the forecourt one late afternoon, playing snowball with the maids and Julian, when two exotic ladies suddenly appeared, Baroness d'Erlanger and her friend Mrs. Lambert. Their car had stuck on the hill in the snow and in their little Bond Street shoes they had picked their way up the hill and through the village. They looked so decorated and artificial, like two paroquettes in our rural black and white Breughel scene.

Their conversation suited their appearance, for it was only about furniture and house decoration. The Baroness d'Erlanger had a very beautiful house in Piccadilly where Byron used to live. I was glad when at last their motor arrived and carried them off, and left me to the peace and silence of our snow world, the green–blue sky and the black trees, and the great log fire in the red room, which filled the house with bitter wood scent.

I remember I was reading then François Villon's poems.

It was about this time that I find this entry in my Journal:

'I went into Oxford to have tea with Aldous Huxley at Balliol as he wanted me to meet some of his friends, Tommy Earp, Harewood and Osmond Grattan Esmonde, who is a descendant of Grattan. He is always called "The Bishop" for he has a fancy to wear a long white cape and large episcopal ring. He is a handsome young man, with an odd, impassive face. He paints pictures of Byzantine saints.

'How very different these young men are to the Cambridge

undergraduates. They seem so soft and effeminate, elegant with gentle affected movements and voices. Tommy Earp is an amusing character, with a high voice and an odd amusing mind. He is very rich and generous. (He is the son of a Newark manufacturer, who married when old to have an heir.)

'In spite of their apparent flippancy and frivolity they are seriously anti-war. They are starting a little magazine, called *The Palatine*, rather precious and literary. I find them rather too exotic, but then I have been reading Roman Rolland's Life of Jaurés, and they seem rather silly compared to him. He was so rugged and fine and courageous and combined intellect and learning with a passionate love of humanity:

> *Son intelligence avait le besoin de l'unité—*
> *et son coeur avait le passion de la Liberté.*
> *Toute intolérence lui faisait horreur.*

A few days later this entry comes:

'D. H. Lawrence, who is in Cornwall, has sent me his "philosophy" to read in MSS. It seems to me deplorable tosh, a volume of words, reiteration, perverted and self-contradictory. A gospel of hate and of violent individualism. He attacks the will, love and sympathy. Indeed, the only thing that he doesn't revile and condemn is love between men and women. But after all what does sexual love lead to, if there is nothing outside to grow out to? For two people, simply to grow in, and in, into each other, does not satisfy a man for long; perhaps a woman might be content, for women are more possessive. I feel very depressed that he has filled himself with these "evening" ideas. They are, I am sure, the outcome of Frieda. Lawrence writes that "They are more married than ever before." I say, "*Voila leur enfant*".

'She will rejoice that I don't like this philosophy, but I cannot pretend to. How Lawrence, as I knew him, who seemed so kind and understanding and essentially so full of tenderness, could turn round and preach this doctrine of hate is difficult to understand, it seems such a complete contradiction of all I found in him and have heard him say.

'But I suppose having accepted Frieda as his wife and finding in her some instinctive satisfaction, he has to suppress his human pity, his gentle and tender qualities, to enable him to fight her and this makes him raw and bitter inside. (The people who are filled with hate must be very unhappy and dissatisfied themselves.)

'More and more I see that the only right attitude is to try and see people with a sight that is clear of personal spite.

'Pure intellect makes a judgement very dry and cruel, and I see that such men are not fit to deal with other human beings; only he that has the warmth of human understanding and is free from self is fitted to judge of others. These go to make the sap that feeds the personality and gives it richness and wisdom, power of growth. Can anyone possess this feeling who turns his back on a spiritual world? I wonder.'

But with Lawrence things were going from bad to worse. Partly owing to the War, which shook him to his depths, for he could not do anything for it or against it. Frieda was German and was being extraordinary tactless and aggressive in the district in Cornwall where they were living, which was by the sea and was specially guarded and supervised.

These two violent creatures were tearing at each other, seeking a harmony that could only be attained if one or other gave up something. He succumbed to her and gave in and as I have said, wrote to me that they were 'really married in spirit now'.

It was this time that he published a book of poems called *Look We Have Come Through*. He came through this very tangled thorny hedge, by leaving part of himself as a tattered garment behind. He and she were there, alone in an enclosure, where they could dance together, mocking and laughing at those outside, calling them fools or enemies.

When Bertie Russell was asked if he had ever read *Look We Have Come Through* his answer was, 'I am glad they have come through, but why should I look?'

Frieda was indeed an extraordinary woman, very vital, robust and virile, a Prussian Brunhilde, who had educated herself on Nietzsche. She was clever in a way but too violent and had no wisdom. She combined timidity with violence, like a great, spoilt, self-willed ungovernable child, who, if she cannot get her own way, will sulk in peevish spiteful temper or steal round and get it another way and then be triumphant.

CHAPTER XII

Bedford Square Again and the First Meeting with the T. S. Eliots. Henry Bentinck and the Russian Officers

In March I went up to London for a few days and joined Philip in Bedford Square. I say in my Journal that 'I felt very much alive and full of excitement at going to London'.

I vividly remember the journey up from Wheatley. Looking out on to the chalk cliffs of Buckinghamshire, the fields just beginning to show a tinge of green, the beech woods and the young trees, tall and slender, making me think of a company of knights with pennants waving in the wind. I imagined all the exciting journeys that one could take if one had an ideal companion such as Keats would have been, who would vibrate and respond to all the wonderful things that one passes as one travels along in life. Most people are so stiff and unresponsive, so absorbed with their own dull lives, that they never seem to realize the electric currents, the exciting things around them, which if they were aware of them might weave new threads into the pattern of their lives. Bertie for instance, never takes any interest in the sights and sounds around him, only in abstract thought. If I go out a walk with him, however much I may be excited or ravished by what I see, it never moves him, he only regards it as a frivolous interruption to some theory he is thinking about.

It was delightful to be back in our dear old house in Bedford Square. We had let off the top floors to Ernest Walkely and only kept the drawing-room and dining-room floors for ourselves, and these in fact were also often 'let'. Bertie Russell was giving some lectures in London and I spent the afternoon with him and then went with Philip to the lecture: The lectures were on War.

My brother Henry came in khaki, and there was a gathering of Bertie's friends, Desmond MacCarthy, the Sangers, Clive Bell and Mrs. Hutchinson and Mark Gertler. It was rather a comic occasion, for all the cranks who attend lectures on any subject

95

were there, and amongst them was a Captain White, who was slightly crazy, and would make a long speech about sex and free love, pointing out that if children were born from parents who were in love with each other they would never want to fight. How would adoring parents ever wish for a war? Then Vernon Lee got up and made a long speech about a cigarette-case, waving her hands about, with her *pince-nez* dangling from it; and of course, a representative of Arts and Crafts made an impassioned harangue—saying that Arts and Crafts alone would cure any tendency to war. Bertie sat looking miserable on the platform. At last he had to ask them to sit down.

Bertie and Desmond came on with me to dinner at Clive Bell's at Gordon Square.

Next evening Philip and I dined with Bertie at a Restaurant in Soho, to meet T. S. Eliot: He is the young American that Bertie met when he was at Harvard in 1914 and thought so clever and overcultured. He had already written some poems, which had appeared in a little American magazine, which Bertie gave me to read; they struck me as very remarkable. He had not long been married and I had not yet met his wife. Bertie had written to me about her and was obviously interested in her. He was convinced that the Eliots were not really happy together, but by a little manipulation on his part everything would come right between them. By what he told me I was not convinced of this and felt doubtful as to whether he would not really make things much worse. Eliot had to return to America to take his degree, but his wife refused to accompany him, as she was afraid of submarines.

The dinner was not a great success. T. S. Eliot was very formal and polite, and his wife seemed to me of the 'spoilt kitten'-type, very second-rate and ultra feminine, playful and naïve, anxious to show she 'possessed' Bertie, when we walked away from the restaurant she headed him off and kept him to herself, walking with him arm-in-arm. I felt rather *froissée* at her bad manners.

Next day I gave a tea-party at Bedford Square. One of the drawing-rooms had been turned into my bedroom. The bed was a large, very high four-poster, with Cardinal-coloured silk curtains, trimmed with silver; it was very lovely looking into that room from the Great Drawing-Room. Molly MacCarthy and Dora Sanger, Brett and Carrington and Gertler and Mr. and Mrs. Eliot and Bertie came. It seemed a happy gay tea-party, at least thus I always remember it. It had the kind of adventurous gaiety that a summer's evening picnic has.

The next evening I dined with Molly and Desmond. Vernon Lee was there and we talked of Henry James and Stendhal. Oh, how I wish I could recall those conversations, beyond these mere names. Desmond, who was in one of his friendly drifting moods, wandered out of his house when I left, and wandered on into my taxi, and wandered still further up to my room at Bedford Square for 'a few moments' as he said. We found in my room 'The bath all prepared before the fire'. 'How comfortable it looks.'

He took up my volume of Villon that I had been reading, and sat down as is his way, forgetful of time, and read poem after poem, with his special and delightful capacity of enjoyment, and on and on we drifted talking of the delights of Poetry.

The next day, Saturday, I returned to Garsington, taking Bertie back with me. Mrs. Hamilton and my brother Henry also came down for the week-end. Henry got on very well with Mrs. Hamilton but found Bertie 'too harsh and pessimistic'.

'Henry always upsets me,' I wrote, 'he seems so poignant and helpless, such an odd combination of extreme censoriousness about people, and woolly-mindedness about general things. I feel he suffers from want of spiritual courage. His real sympathies are with the Peace Party, but Birdie's influence and that of all his smart friends would prevent him from openly declaring himself. He is also afraid to go under the surface of life, and covers up anything that seems ugly or dishonourable, and calls me "degenerate".

'I do not understand why, but I think it is a word the smart people use for anyone who is different from themselves, or who cares for Art or for what lies behind the externals of life. Everything seems to me to have an inner soul. When Julian and Lalage dance I want them to express the idea of what they are dancing, not only the outer clothes and dressing up. Even when one reads a book I feel one must try and feel the essence of thought in it, not only the words. Precious things are not obvious, one must seek further. Almost everything worth knowing is hidden, intricate, subtle. That is why it is foolish to judge unless one has seen the hidden side.'

On Saturday, March 19, Maynard Keynes and Lytton and Norton came for the week-end and it seemed a very happy party.

We all knew each other so well and were familiar and few, and I didn't feel anxious or worried, but could let myself be natural and gay.

On the Sunday morning Boris Anrep arrived with two Russian officers. They were dressed up in grand uniforms and high Russian boots, and were as proud as peacocks, strutting about showing off their fine figures. I could not bear them for underneath I saw that they were brutal and savage. They laughed at the idea of atrocities. 'Of course, every side did such things and burnt and pillaged wherever they went.' It is of course more honest than our own high fallutin ideas of war, but it left me speechless.

I hardly recognized Boris, who used to be so charming and simple and full of fun, a real gay artist. Now he seemed a great red-faced brutal fellow, puffed up with pride at being a Captain. I was thankful when the time came for them to leave.

As they drove off a motor arrived with Sir John Simon and his two daughters and a governess. He is always thought 'so able', 'so clever', but his manner is so formal and so insincerely polite and condescending that he completely baffled me. He smiles and smiles and bows his head and I murmur to myself, 'Serpent'. When he came into our lovely red panelled room, he looked round with a condescending smile and said, 'How amusing'. I unfortunately had a piece of wax in one ear which made me completely deaf on that side. Maynard had to keep poking me at tea saying, 'Sir John is talking to you, Ottoline.'

Then came a visit from Helen Dudley, Bertie's old love from America.

'A queer creature,' I wrote. 'So lethargic and feline. She must be a strange descendant of vampires, though I don't feel she is really evil now. I suppose having lived so long in civilized society has taken the sting out of her. She sits and looks into the fire for hours and seems to be remembering sadly what a wonderful time vampires had in old days before they had strayed into this degenerate intellectual world. She seems to be trying to accustom herself to talk, and she does so by repeating after one what one has said, then she will go on and on and learn what the next person says. She is really only a vampire of ideas and sentences. Meanwhile her body is laced and anaemic. What she really needs is blood, not ideas and words.'

March 26 1916.

'The ——s are here. How I suffer under them! She is so managing, so judging. She seems to intrude so clumsily into my affairs, fingers everything, and would like to finger my inner life as she fingers my books.

'She is terrified of ideas. The only world these managing, family ladies know is the practical, fussy, managing world. The only world I want to know is the world of ideas and imagination, truth of thought, truth as to life. We grow further and further apart and speak different languages. When she talks of things that I like I cannot bear it and shrink away. Sometimes I feel that I have a terrible strength inside me and that if I let it I could crush anyone, but I withhold it and keep it in bondage, for I know what affects other people is not only words, what one says, but the inner attitude of thoughts and feelings. There is something primitive in me that asserts itself in a desire to lash some people round with a whip of scorn; curl it round them as my mother taught me her father had seen the priests in Ireland do with their riding whips to girls when they had failed to go to confession. But once one allowed that to happen, all would be wrecked inside one and I am thankful that generally my love curls round them and I feel only compassion and affection. I feel sorry for —— in a way, for she says she hasn't many friends, only her children, and she is so absorbed with food and material things, that she doesn't try and keep her mind alert.

'The only thing that —— could find to talk to me about was my income. As we walked down through the fields to the wood to look for the daffodils he asked me, "How is your income?" I was nonplussed. I could only answer, "I really don't know. Philip looks after that. I expect it is very bad, but I find the only way is not to think about it."

'Dear, Oh dear. I shall be glad when they go. One of their great faults is their want of humour. Oh! How exhausting and difficult visitors are, but I can always hide in my little room. It is lovely and comforting to be there alone with all my books round me. They are the companions that I love best. With human beings one wants so much time, circling round and round things, talking banalities before one can light the spark that sets up any contact. But here in my little room I am happy, for it is a sanctuary from all the agitations and annoyances outside. As I shut my door and lean my back against it I feel a thrill of delight to find myself here in shelter. The grey-blue walls, and Duncan's picture, and the gay colours of the cushions, all yellow and orange and pink, gay and full of joy, and the sunshine of Italy which still lives in the bits of old brocade. My books too, dressed in their bright green and yellow bindings.

Stendhal says that a *roman* is like the strings and bridge of a violin and the case is the soul of the reader. My little room is my soul's outer case and shares with me the feelings and thoughts that vibrate through me.

'Here I have talked to those I most care for, written to them and read their letters. Here in the evenings alone I sit with the yellow-shaded lamps and read and dream and work out my life; and now, sitting by the fire of wood which flares up red and green and orange, and sends out a strong pungent smell, the smell of the sap that has come out of the earth. These were young trees that are burning now for their scent is green and bitter. Life burns me and wrings me; what Incense do I give out in its fire? I wonder. I should like it to be of Iris, strong and pure.

'Now my fire smells of cherries, perhaps that last log was a cherry tree.'

CHAPTER XIII

The Prime Minister and a Plea for Conscientious Objectors

'March ended with a terrible blizzard, snow and an angry, wailing, screaming storm. When I was out walking, the rain and snow drove me along and I could hardly bear its lashings on my face, as I came home round the bend in the road. I found one of the large trees had fallen across the road, breaking down the wall by the Monastic buildings. Julian and Lalage (her little companion) had only passed by two minutes before. It made me sick to think of it. I imagined them lying under it! All the farm men are busy now with saws, cutting it up. It was hollow inside.

'Lytton has just left us (but he soon returned). He was here for some weeks, sympathetic and charming all the time. I had wonderful talks with him about every kind of subject—Politics, Poetry, Shelley and Wordsworth, Congreve, Racine, Blake. He is very unhappy about the conscientious objectors. Bertie Russell came down for the Sunday. He is working furiously at the No Conscription Fellowship, very exalted and delirious about them all, Thinking they are really wonderful, as I am sure they are, True and firm and gaily courageous. It is splendid that Bertie is helping them, for he will gain faith from knowing such fine gay men, and his influence will strengthen them.

'I never feel my best with Bertie. I cannot tell why. He always quenches my light-heartedness and gaiety and puts a blight on me. T. S. Eliot, his American poet friend came with him. I was very excited that T. S. Eliot was coming with him, but I found him dull, dull, dull. He never moves his lips but speaks in an even and monotonous voice, and I felt him monotonous without and within. Where does his queer neurasthenic poetry come from, I wonder. From his New England, Puritan inheritance and upbringing? I think he has lost all spontaneity and can only break through his conventionality by stimulants or violent emotions. He is obviously very ignorant of England and imagines that it is essential to be highly polite and conventional and decorous, and meticulous. I tried to get him to talk more freely by talking French to him, as I thought he might feel freer doing so, but I don't think it was a great success, although better than English. He speaks French very perfectly, slowly and correctly. As I remember this I feel how odd it was, but it shows how very foreign Eliot seemed to me then; but I generally found that Americans are as foreign to us as Germans are.

'I think Lytton liked him but was as puzzled by him as I was.'

At Easter we had another party. Molly MacCarthy, Clive Bell, Mrs. Hutchinson, Roger Fry, Norton, and Maria Nys was with us from Cambridge. We had talks, talks, walks in the wood and a tea picnic there on Sunday, as it was lovely spring weather.

After tea Molly, Maria and I walked over to Cuddesdon to hear Bishop Gore preach. It was always an event to me hearing him, for he is unusual, sincere and holy.

On Monday afternoon a huge motor arrived at the gates. I saw a very large, fat lady getting out and then a thin one, and then I realized that Violet Asquith was already walking across the forecourt. I ran down to tell the maid Daisy to admit them and as I passed the window again I saw the Prime Minister. I ran and told Philip and our guests, who, I think, were having a rest, and begged them to come and help me entertain the invaders.

For a time it seemed a turmoil. The Asquiths all talking shrilly against each other. Margot's and Violet's voices above the others. I asked Philip to take the screaming company over the house.

I now cannot remember who the fat lady was—perhaps Mrs. George Keppel. I took the old man to my sitting-room, as I was anxious to talk to him about conscientious objectors. I began by talking of books, Stendhal, etc., and then I plunged into the subject that I had so much on my mind, and about which I was trembling inside, knowing that he could affect the lives of hundreds of young men.

I started by saying, 'You know I am a rebel! I am passionately in sympathy with the conscientious objectors.'

Once this plunge was made I went on to tell him all about them, especially about some who were under a severe penalty—I believe the death sentence.

He asked many questions and seemed impressed and sympathetic. I was very frank and explicit as I say in my Journal. He on his side abused Military People.

After this rather nerve-wrecking conversation was over, we relapsed into sentimentalizing, and talking over old days, when he used to come and see me in what he called 'My Tower' in Grosvenor Place. I was always fond of the old man, and would like to have renewed friendship with him, but I don't believe he has *affection* for those that he has been attracted to sentimentally and physically. I feel that he is always a spectator in life and doesn't really feel the War or anything else very deeply.

On May 2nd I wrote:

'All last week it was divinely beautiful. The spring coming all in a rush. Apple and Pear blossom and the Tulips and Narcissus just out.

'Our Easter guests all went off on Tuesday and Maria back to Cambridge. Bertie arrived on Friday, very full of his C.O. work and very happy, quite a changed man, for he is using up all his activities, no surplus left over to go bad. I hope it will last, for it makes him so happy. I think if he can keep up his present enthusiasm he may really lead a movement.

'On Sunday Margot Asquith sent over her motor to take us all over to The Wharf for tea, Philip and me, Julian and Lalage. When we arrived we found that the Prime Minister had gone out, which disappointed me. Gilbert Murray was just leaving. Philip had had a long talk with him the day before in Oxford and had begged him to see the Prime Minister about the conscientious objectors. He said when we met him that he had had a satisfactory talk with him. Margot talked to me a long time about Lady Glenconner and Sir Edward Grey, and about my brother Henry. She was in love with him, I believe, in old days. She added that Asquith was really devoted to me, and that he always said that I was a "remarkable woman".

'Diana Manners and Violet Bonham Carter were there. All these people seem curiously apart from real life, as if they had no comprehension of what goes on except in their own little Set.

'Violet seemed depressed.

'The position of the Government is very precarious.'

CHAPTER XIV

Lytton Strachey

Lytton was still with us in March (1917). He had been up to have his medical examination at the White City. He told us that he had waited there from 11 to 3.30, reading Gardiner's *History of England*. He was then examined by an R.A.M.C. orderly. He undressed with three other young men, rough fellows, and then appeared naked before the Doctor. One of the young Doctors burst out laughing when he saw him, and no wonder, for he must have looked a very odd sight amongst the other strong sturdy fellows, he so tall and emaciated, with his long beard. They exempted him entirely.

I find in my Journal this entry:

'I enjoy Lytton's visit immensely. He does not get up until late, and has breakfast in bed every morning. So I go up after breakfast to enquire after his health and sit on his bed and we have wonderful talks.

'One morning it was about his love affairs, casual and serious. Apparently he finds a number of young people in London quite willing to respond to his advances, and he says they have charming relations together. We both said what a pity it was that so many years of our lives had been dumb to all "experiences", and through shyness or prudery we had always withdrawn.

'Sometimes when I am in calm waters I long for adventures, but then when I think about them and realize all that they entail, I know that I am too fastidious and always have been to enjoy agitations, passions. Of all men, and indeed of all people, Lytton is entirely the easiest to talk to, for, though very selfish, he is not egotistical, indeed, he is most sympathetic with charming humour and a love of poking fun, which is very stimulating to my love of fantastic confessions and descriptions. Since I overcame my shyness with him there is no one that I enjoy talking to as I do with him, although we differ on many things, especially religion. His love of poetry and good literature is unequalled.'

Now that he is dead I never cease to miss him, and how often do I find myself thinking, 'I must write and tell Lytton about this.'

He was at this time greatly interested in a new Life of Words-worth by an American called Harper—a history of Wordsworth's early life in France—when he was strongly opposed to our war with France.

Lytton admires Wordsworth's sister Dorothy very much. All his poems to Lucy are apparently to her.

Her journal he thinks very fine, simple but full of wonderful sentences.

CHAPTER XV

Rescue of a Land Girl from the Pond by Robert Ross

Towards the end of May, Violet Bonham Carter came to stay with us for a week-end. She had suggested coming and I had tried to put her off, without success. I asked Lytton and Maynard Keynes and Desmond MacCarthy and a young Mr. Winterton (a conscientious objector) to meet her.

Henry, my brother, had been to see me for the day on Saturday, but had to leave very soon after tea. I went to the door to say good-bye and see him off, as I always did, and left Violet and Lytton sitting side by side at the long tea table in the red room. When I came back I found Lytton was alone. I laughingly said, 'What have you done with Violet?' and I pretended to look under the table for her. Lytton, I thought, looked slightly upset. He held up his long hands and whispered in his high voice, 'She has fled upstairs to her room!'

I saw that something had happened. After I left them Violet had started to abuse conscientious objectors, although she knew quite well that we all at Garsington were their supporters, and that Lytton himself was one. She said they disgraced England and ought to be deported to a desert island.

This naturally annoyed Lytton and he answered, 'If these are the Government's views I don't see much difference between them and the Prussians.'

This made her very angry, for she became very red and gathered up her bag and gloves with an angry wave of her hand and swept out of the room.

I felt very much annoyed with her, for she knew quite well the opinions of those she would meet if she came to us; but to her any criticism of the Government is a personal criticism. I was puzzled to know what to do. Did she mean to leave the house? Anyhow it was not a pleasant start to a week-end. I went up to her bedroom and found her there still flushed and angry, but I made no reference to the scene, and suggested that she should come for a walk. That walk was not a very happy one.

It was indeed a godsend that Desmond MacCarthy was with us, for he is always like oil on any troubled waters. Lytton told him of the scene; he and Maynard carried us through the week-end. But she never addressed a word to Lytton while she was in the house. Since those days, after Lytton became famous, Violet tried to make up to him. I don't know whether he responded. I know I should have said, 'Too late, too late.'

In the evening, after dinner, she talked everyone down, in a very irritating manner. She seemed quite unaccustomed carrying on a discussion on equality; if she is answered she gets angry. She is very glib but not really very intelligent. She is quite nice when she talks of her father or of her brother Cys, to whom she is devoted, but her talk makes me feel life is dust and ashes, as if it were all made up of words and sentences.

The following Sunday Clive Bell, Carrington, Brett and Lytton were still with us. As it was a lovely hot day we took our tea down to the wood to have a picnic there. In the morning we had been bathing in the pond, and as we were to be out in the after-noon I gave permission for the maids to bathe. At that time we had a land girl called Lucy to act as groom, a pretty, fair-haired and attractive girl. She had boasted of having won swimming medals and life saving diplomas, and as the pond was not deep I thought it quite safe to let them bathe.

While we were happily enjoying our tea all spread out in the wood, a breathless maid arrived, running from the house to call me back. She was very agitated, very out of breath, and kept telling me an incoherent story of 'Lucy drowning', 'The Prime Minister arriving', and a gentleman 'plunging into the pond.'

I started off to run the mile or so across cowslip fields home. I found that the Prime Minister and all his party had already left, and from Eva, my maid, who was in a state of great agitation and nerves, I disentangled what had happened. The maids had been bathing very happily when they saw arriving on the lawn the Prime Minister and a party of friends (Edwin Montague, Mrs. George Keppel, Elizabeth Asquith[1] and Robbie Ross). Suddenly Lucy called out that she was drowning. The gallant Robbie Ross threw his precious presentation watch aside and

[1] She later became Princess Antoine Bibesco, and published some fiction.